Sweet Treats

A Collection of Designs for Beaded Jewellery and Gifts to Make your Mouth Water

KATIE DEAN

This book is dedicated to my friends and family with thanks for their love and support. Also to David, Siobhan and the many people out there for whom CFS/ME presents huge daily challenges. I hope each one of you finds your own path to recovery.

Published by Tregellas Publishing

page 6

Before You Start

Recipes

page 30

CONTENTS

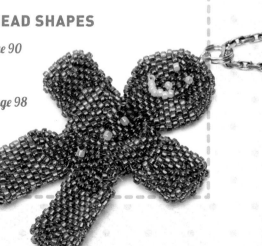

INTRODUCTION

This book started life as a sequel to my first book which featured miniature celebration cakes. I wanted to develop my cake theme to incorporate cakes and desserts that would make distinctive beadwork. I also wanted to play around with some ideas for making cake-related jewellery as well as ornamental gifts. However, what started out as a simple idea, has undergone just as much of a journey as I have done personally.

I started beading seriously soon after I was diagnosed with ME, or Chronic Fatigue Syndrome. The beading was a natural progression of my lifelong love of craftwork, but during my illness it became a therapy. It provided me with a distraction that was creative, allowed me to feel a sense of achievement and gave my life back some of the purpose that it had lost. More importantly, the meditative nature of beading, I believe, proved to be instrumental in my recovery. Also instrumental in that recovery process has been the amazing support of my family and friends.

On a personal level, this book became a project related to my recovery process. When I started out I did not think that I would recover as well as I have done. I am still on the road to full recovery, but the progress I have made whilst working on this project has been enormous. I wanted to do something to mark the support that friends and family have demonstrated, so after coming up with a few ideas, I decided to involve some friends. In April 2011 I sent a message to a small selection of friends who have also supported my beadwork, requesting some ideas for cakes and sweet treats. They came up with some great responses as you will see from the projects in here.

The suggestions from friends provided some excellent challenges, allowing me to develop my thoughts on three-dimensional designing with beads. I started thinking about the different ways in which one can replicate real objects in beads and it soon became clear to me that I was using five basic concepts: bead colour, bead size, bead type, bead stitches, bead shapes. I deliberately pursued this idea to create five sections for this book which I hope will help you think about some of the different 'tools', in terms of concepts and ideas, that you can use in developing new designs.

Finally, a chance question about the origin of chocolate dipped strawberries piqued my curiosity. I started seeking an answer to that question and then thought that it would be good fun to find out a little about the origins of all my sweet treats. The results are included at the start of each project. There are some great stories, which I like to hope are true, but please don't quote me – this is just a little bit of fun, not a serious piece of research! The baking times for each recipe are also a bit of fun designed to follow the 'recipe book' theme. They will vary depending on your level of experience, but should give an indication of whether each project is long or short.

This book is designed for people who have some experience of beading. Part one provides a brief guide to the different stitches I have used in the projects, but does not aim to teach the techniques from scratch. For best results, please make sure that you have a good understanding of the techniques before you embark upon the projects in part two.

Finally, I hope that working through this book will provide you with as much fun and inspiration as I have found in writing it.

Before you start

CHAPTER 1

BEADING BASICS

In this chapter I will be sharing some of the tips I have learnt over the years. If you are new to beading, this is essential reading: it is important to develop good habits as soon as you start. You will find that using good working practices makes your beading time more enjoyable. For those of you who are already experienced, it is worth reminding yourselves of the basics before you get started on the recipes in this book.

Liquorice Allsorts Necklace

My Liquorice Allsorts pendant is one of my first food-based designs – I love these sweets and had fun with the colours and shapes. The leather cord reminded me of a string of liquorice so provided the perfect finishing touch.

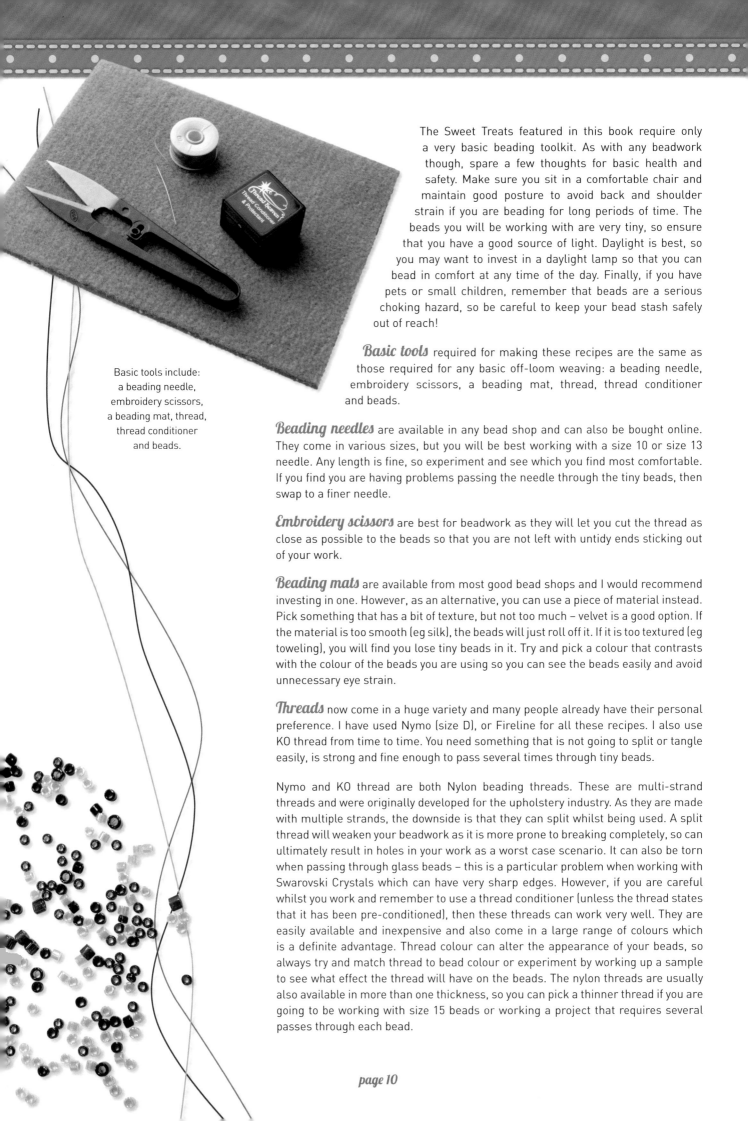

The Sweet Treats featured in this book require only a very basic beading toolkit. As with any beadwork though, spare a few thoughts for basic health and safety. Make sure you sit in a comfortable chair and maintain good posture to avoid back and shoulder strain if you are beading for long periods of time. The beads you will be working with are very tiny, so ensure that you have a good source of light. Daylight is best, so you may want to invest in a daylight lamp so that you can bead in comfort at any time of the day. Finally, if you have pets or small children, remember that beads are a serious choking hazard, so be careful to keep your bead stash safely out of reach!

Basic tools include: a beading needle, embroidery scissors, a beading mat, thread, thread conditioner and beads.

Basic tools required for making these recipes are the same as those required for any basic off-loom weaving: a beading needle, embroidery scissors, a beading mat, thread, thread conditioner and beads.

Beading needles are available in any bead shop and can also be bought online. They come in various sizes, but you will be best working with a size 10 or size 13 needle. Any length is fine, so experiment and see which you find most comfortable. If you find you are having problems passing the needle through the tiny beads, then swap to a finer needle.

Embroidery scissors are best for beadwork as they will let you cut the thread as close as possible to the beads so that you are not left with untidy ends sticking out of your work.

Beading mats are available from most good bead shops and I would recommend investing in one. However, as an alternative, you can use a piece of material instead. Pick something that has a bit of texture, but not too much – velvet is a good option. If the material is too smooth (eg silk), the beads will just roll off it. If it is too textured (eg toweling), you will find you lose tiny beads in it. Try and pick a colour that contrasts with the colour of the beads you are using so you can see the beads easily and avoid unnecessary eye strain.

Threads now come in a huge variety and many people already have their personal preference. I have used Nymo (size D), or Fireline for all these recipes. I also use KO thread from time to time. You need something that is not going to split or tangle easily, is strong and fine enough to pass several times through tiny beads.

Nymo and KO thread are both Nylon beading threads. These are multi-strand threads and were originally developed for the upholstery industry. As they are made with multiple strands, the downside is that they can split whilst being used. A split thread will weaken your beadwork as it is more prone to breaking completely, so can ultimately result in holes in your work as a worst case scenario. It can also be torn when passing through glass beads – this is a particular problem when working with Swarovski Crystals which can have very sharp edges. However, if you are careful whilst you work and remember to use a thread conditioner (unless the thread states that it has been pre-conditioned), then these threads can work very well. They are easily available and inexpensive and also come in a large range of colours which is a definite advantage. Thread colour can alter the appearance of your beads, so always try and match thread to bead colour or experiment by working up a sample to see what effect the thread will have on the beads. The nylon threads are usually also available in more than one thickness, so you can pick a thinner thread if you are going to be working with size 15 beads or working a project that requires several passes through each bead.

Fireline is one of the bonded beading threads. These were originally developed as fishing line for sportsmen, but someone realised that they made excellent beading thread. Bonded threads tend to create a slightly stiffer piece of beadwork, so that can be an advantage for a lot of these recipes. It is also very difficult to split a bonded thread and I have always found that if they do tangle into a knot, it is very easy to undo the knot without splitting or damaging the thread. Some people advocate conditioning bonded thread as well, but I have not found this to be necessary. Unfortunately bonded threads are significantly more expensive than the nylon alternative. They are also only commonly available in a small range of colours. I tend to use the crystal as I find that it is fairly unobtrusive and seems to tone well with most beads, but try experimenting for yourself.

Thread conditioner is not essential, but is strongly advisable if you choose to work with a nylon thread. I use Thread Heaven. When you have cut your length of thread, take one end, hold it in place on the conditioner using your thumb, then pull the end so that the full length of thread passes across the conditioner, under your thumb. Conditioner helps to keep the thread supple and stop it from splitting and twisting or knotting and generally saves a lot of frustration!

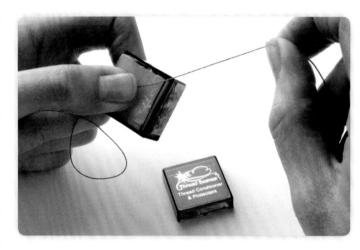

Condition thread by passing it across the thread conditioner

Beads come in all shapes and sizes as you know. These recipes all use Delica beads, sometimes with a mix of seed beads for some of the elements. Most of the recipes are made using Peyote stitch and I find that the Delicas, because of their regular shape, create the most uniform Peyote. I sometimes elect to use seed beads instead because I know they will be a little less uniform, so the resulting beadwork will be less structured, which can be an advantage for some elements of the recipe. In many cases the size or colour (or both) of the bead are critical to the recipe design, so do follow the recommendations in the ingredients for each recipe. I have tried to indicate when the recipe will work with a different bead size, for example using a size 15 bead instead of a size 11 so that you can make matching earrings. It is always interesting to try experimenting and see what will happen if you try following the pattern using a different type of bead – many an interesting idea has developed that way – so once you understand how a recipe works, do feel free to try some alternatives if you are feeling curious.

GENERAL WORKING TIPS

If you are an experienced beader, you will probably have developed or been taught your own favourite methods for adding new threads, finishing off ends and so forth. If you are still learning, then in this section I will try and pass on methods that I have found work for me. Every beading book you read will suggest something different, so always remain open to change and experiment to find out what produces the best results and makes you feel comfortable.

Thread length is quite a personal preference. If you use a length of thread that is too short, you will find yourself constantly having to join new threads which is fiddly and also makes the beadwork less strong. Every time you add a new thread you are potentially creating an area of weakness where the beads could pull apart from each other more easily. On the other hand, if you use a length of thread that is too long, you will struggle to pull it through the beads comfortably and it is more likely to become tangled. Personally I find a length of roughly a full armspan is about right.

Knotting between beads is an essential, but thankfully simple, skill.

Step 1: After you have exited a bead, pass your needle underneath the thread that sits between the bead you have just exited and its immediate neighbour.

Step 2: Pull your needle through until you have a small loop of thread between the two beads.

Step 3: Pass the needle through this loop of thread

Step 4: Pull the needle so that the threads tighten and knot. The knot should be sitting invisibly between your two beads. As you continue stitching, the motion of pulling the thread should move the knot into a bead and completely out of sight.

Joining new thread is going to be inevitable for some of these recipes since they require too long a length to be able to complete with a single piece of thread. Cut a length of thread with which you are comfortable working. Pass through three beads two or three rows below, but close to the bead from which you need to continue working. Leave a tiny tail which you can cut off later, knot between beads and then pass your needle through your beadwork until you reach the bead from which you wish to continue working. NB as you pass through beads, make sure your thread keeps to the pattern of the stitch ie for peyote stitch, the thread moves diagonally between beads, not directly up and down. Thread paths can show if they diverge from the correct pattern and this makes the beadwork look untidy.

Finishing off old thread is basically the same principle as joining new thread, but in reverse. As the piece of thread you are using becomes too short to continue stitching, pass it down through a few beads to exit from a bead a few rows below the point at which you are working. Knot between beads and then continue passing your thread through a few more beads. You can repeat the knots every few beads for added security. Remember to keep the thread path in line with the correct pattern for your stitch.

Trim thread ends as close to the beadwork as possible so that they don't show. It is best to pull the end hard and, as you trim close to the beads, it should then spring back slightly to settle inside a bead and out of sight. If your beadwork has a right and a wrong side, try and keep all thread ends exiting from the wrong side so that if they do work their way out of the bead, they won't show. You may also like to add a tiny dab of 'Fray Check' to the end of the thread after you have trimmed it. This will help it to stick inside a bead and not pull out later on as you are working. Fray Check has been developed for use by the textiles industry to help stop material from fraying. It is available from craft shops or sewing shops and may be sold under different brand names.

Working with Beads is easiest if you establish a few basic practises for organising your working space. When you are using multiple colours or types of beads, separate each different type into a distinct pile. These recipes all use letters to label the beads and then refer to the letters in the instructions. Use a small piece of paper to write a label for each pile and then you will know exactly which beads you need to pick up as you work.

If you are working from a pattern that refers to the bead type rather than a letter, then write this on the piece of paper. Find a method that will allow you to quickly identify the beads you need to use. You may want to just create piles of beads on your beading mat, or you can use a shallow upturned lid for each variety of bead so that the piles of beads are completely separated and will not roll into one another as you work.

Each recipe also gives the number of beads required in each row. It is easiest if you separate out the beads you will need for a row before you start working on that particular row. That way, if you reach the end of the row and find that you either have beads left over, or are short of beads, you will immediately know that you have made a mistake. You can check this and correct it as you go rather than finding out in several rows' time when you will need to undo a lot of work.

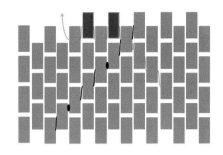

STARTING AND FINISHING THREADS
Dots illustrate the knots between beads. Black lines and dots illustrate the path for finishing a thread. Green lines and dots indicate the path for starting a new thread, with brown beads showing the continuation of stitching.

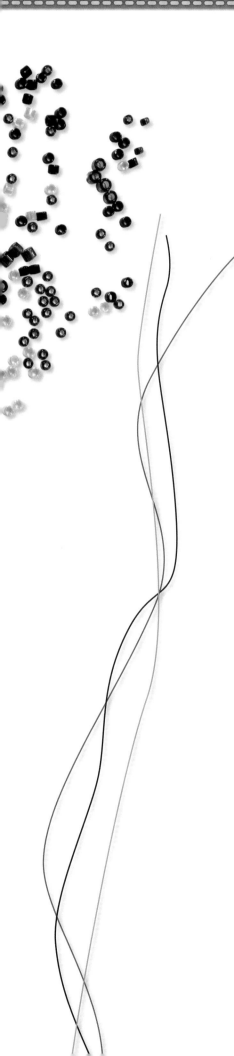

CORRECTING MISTAKES

Even the most experienced beader will make mistakes, but the skill is not so much in avoiding them as in learning how to correct them properly. This may sound like hard work, but remember, nothing is beyond repair. At worst, follow the tradition of Native American beaders: they would create a deliberate mistake (usually an incorrectly coloured bead referred to as a 'Spirit Bead') in every piece of beadwork as a reminder that no mortal thing is perfect.

Split thread can create big problems as it can weaken your beadwork. If you find that you have split a thread, unthread your needle, remove the beads as far back as a point a few beads before the split occurred, stitch the thread in to finish it off and then begin a new thread. Even if the beadwork seems secure at the time, the split thread will be a weak point that can cause breakages later, which is even more annoying than pausing to start the new thread at the time.

Knotted thread is a common problem. Rather than tugging at the knot, which can just cause it to tighten further, carefully use a needle and insert it into the centre of the knot, then gently wiggle it around until the knot begins to loosen and you can see how to untangle it. Be careful not to split the thread as you do this. As a last resort, just cut your thread before the knot and continue working.

Frog stitch or 'rip it, rip it' is something that most beaders will need to become skilled at practising! I most often realise that I've made a mistake when I reach the same point in the following row of beadwork. The only way to correct it is to undo the beadwork all the way back around the row I have just stitched, to the point where I went wrong. When you do this, always remove your needle and undo your work by easing up the last bead stitched until you can unpick the thread, so you will work backwards one bead at a time. If you try and stitch back through your work removing beads, you are likely to either split your thread as you go or find that your needle has passed through the bead along a different path and the bead you are trying to remove is in fact now stitched double into your work. If there is some critical reason for not removing the needle, then pass it back through the work eye end first as this is slightly less likely to split threads, but I do not recommend this.

Picking up the wrong bead is very easy to do and can be very annoying. It is avoidable if you are working in good light and paying attention as you go, but it will still happen from time to time. If you notice in time, you can unpick the beadwork back to the rogue bead and correct the mistake. If you only notice after finishing the piece, then your best option may be to simply leave it as a spirit bead!

How to break a bead. Usually I would not advocate breaking beads, but there are times when this is the only way to remove a rogue bead from your work. The danger is that in breaking the bead, you also break the thread or wire on which the bead is sitting and then your work will fall apart. However, if you carefully place a pair of pliers so that they sit on the top and bottom of the bead, not around the middle, and then crush the bead between them, you should avoid breaking the thread at the same time. Remember to close your eyes or use protective goggles as you crush the bead – it will probably result in tiny pieces of glass flying in different directions and you do not want to end up with any of them in your eyes! As a general rule, I would only use this method of correction as a very last resort. It can be more applicable when French beading or doing bead crochet than off-loom weaving.

FOLLOWING A PEYOTE STITCH PATTERN

Whilst many sets of instructions will tell you which beads to pick up in which order for each row that you stitch, sometimes it is easier to follow a diagram or pattern. This is especially true if you are creating a piece of flat peyote that has a picture, pattern or writing on it. Although there is still likely to be accompanying text to tell you how many beads in a row and how many rows you will be stitching, you will need to work out the placement of different coloured beads for yourself, so here are a few tips. If you still find that you cannot follow the rows in Peyote stitch, just turn the pattern at a ninety degree angle and you will be able to work it up in brick stitch. It is easier to distinguish the rows from one another when viewed this way around.

Start out by stringing the beads that will complete the first two rows of your pattern. In the example in the photo, these are all dark pink beads (top). As you add the next (third) row, you will start to form the up and down pattern of peyote stitch. In this instance, these are all the silver beads. Look carefully at the example and make sure you are happy that you can distinguish which row is which and would be able to count the rows if necessary (there are 17 rows in this piece)

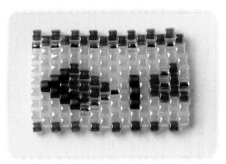

Peyote Pattern

Pick out the pattern by isolating key beads. In this instance, look for the difference between rows that are made up with all the same colour beads and rows that contain a mix of different colour beads. After your row of silver beads, you would stitch 3 rows of pale pink beads. In the next row you add 1 dark pink bead that forms the top point of the diamond

Use 'Reference Points' as you go along to create the pattern, whether it be a picture, a shape or a number. The dark pink bead forms an easy reference point – you can see that in the next row you will add a black bead on one side of this bead and another dark pink bead on the other. You should also notice that you need to stitch your second 'reference point' in this row – the top dark pink bead in the shape on the right of the piece. In this way you should be able to see where you are relative to the pattern instead of keep having to count which row you are on and how many beads to stitch.

Marking the Pattern is essential unless it is small enough to work up in a single session. Different people have different preferences for this. You can use sticky notes to mark the point you have reached. This can be useful as you can write notes on them as well so that you remember what you were planning to do next. Some people like to photocopy the pattern and make notes straight onto it, perhaps colouring in the bead where they finished working. You can place the pattern in a plastic page protector and then use a marker to write on the plastic, rather than writing directly onto the pattern. I have watched beaders use a pin to stick into the pattern as they work so that they do not lose track of the row on which they are working. If you are happy to spend a little money, then a lot of craft stores sell magnetic boards. These are basically a metal board with a magnet across it, so you can place the pattern on the board and then move the magnet to mark your place as you work. If you do not already have a favourite practise, then try a few different ideas and see what works best for you.

COPYRIGHT

Every beader needs to be aware of the basics when it comes to copyright. The designer auto-matically holds the copyright to their own work and it is a legal offence for anyone else to make up the designer's pattern and sell it as their own. By making designs public, the designer gives their permission for others to use those designs for personal use. As soon as you start creating your own designs and realize the amount of work involved, you will understand why it is so frustrating to have someone else come along and use all your hard work and pass it off as their own. Not to mention, a design is a very personal reflection of you. However, it can be hard to determine when you start infringing copyright. If you make up someone else's design in a different colour, or with slight changes, you are starting to overlay your own design work, so would it then be alright to pass it off as your own? This is a complex subject, but the best rule of thumb is to observe some common courtesy – if in doubt, contact the designer, state what you want to do and ask if they mind. In the beading world, as in any other artistic world, advances are made through mutual respect and collaboration – any artist will be inspired by and grow through understanding and developing the work of their fellow artists, but we also need to retain respect for the hard work of our fellows.

CHAPTER 2

BEADING TECHNIQUES

This chapter gives a very quick overview of the different beading techniques that you will be using in the following recipes. It is not intended to be used as a tool for learning these techniques. There are many excellent books and online tutorials already available for that purpose. So if you are a beginner, I would recommend that you first familiarise yourself with the basic beading techniques, either by teaching yourself from printed material or by joining a beading group or local beading class. I hope that the following pages will provide a useful reminder of how the different techniques work and that you will be able to flick back to this chapter as you need to when working on the various cake recipes.

Pick 'n Mix Necklace
I decided to try and limit myself to a simple colour scheme of pink, yellow and brown whilst creating a necklace on the theme of different sweets.

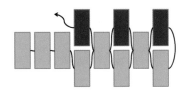

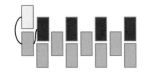

EVEN COUNT STRAIGHT PEYOTE STITCH

EVEN COUNT STRAIGHT PEYOTE STITCH

Begin by picking up an even number of beads. This will create the first two rows of your strip of Peyote stitch.

Pick up a bead and pass back through the second to last bead in your strip.

Pick up a bead and pass through the next but one bead in your strip. Repeat this process until you reach the end of the strip. This completes row 3 (brown).

For even count Peyote, when you reach the end of the current row (brown) you will see that you are exiting from the final bead in the previous row (pink). To begin the next row, pick up a new bead (yellow) and pass through the last bead from the current row (brown). Continue working back and forth this way until you have the desired number of rows.

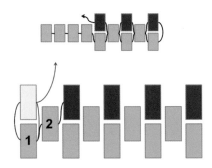

ODD COUNT STRAIGHT PEYOTE STITCH

ODD COUNT STRAIGHT PEYOTE STITCH

Pick up an odd number of beads to form your first two rows. Complete row 3 as you did for even count Peyote stitch. The turn at the end of the row is different.

When you add the penultimate bead from row 3, pass through the last two beads in your base strip (black stitching line through beads labelled '1' and '2'). Pick up the final row 3 bead (shown in yellow), pass back through bead '1' and through the final row 3 bead (yellow) so that you are exiting ready to continue with row 4 of your strip. This is referred to as the square stitch turn because you are stitching the final bead of the row using square stitch.

When you reach the end of row 4, the turn to begin row 5 is the same as for the even count variation. Continue, alternating turning techniques, until you have the required number of rows.

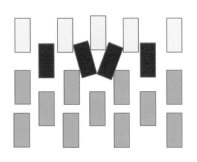

PEYOTE STITCH INCREASE

PEYOTE STITCH INCREASE

The Peyote stitch increase is completed over the course of two rows – an increase row and a straight row to confirm the increase.

First Row: When you reach the point at which you wish to increase, pick up two beads instead of one and pass through the next bead to continue stitching along the row.

Second Row: When you reach the point at which you added two beads, add a bead in between the pair of beads. This forces the beadwork to widen and completes your increase. It is however, still a 'straight' row of Peyote since it is adding one bead in every space.

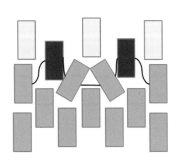

PEYOTE STITCH DECREASE

PEYOTE STITCH DECREASE

The Peyote stitch decrease is completed over the course of two rows – a decrease row and a straight row to confirm the decrease.

First Row: When you reach the point at which you wish to decrease, pass through two beads instead of adding a new bead between them as you would for straight Peyote.

Second row: When you reach the point where you created the start of the decrease, add a single bead over the top of the pair that are pulled together. This will pull the Peyote stitch inwards and complete the decrease. It is however, still a 'straight' row of Peyote since it is adding one bead in every space.

TWO DROP PEYOTE STITCH

This is exactly the same as normal Peyote, but instead of picking up one bead and passing through one bead, you will pick up two beads and pass through two beads. It can be used to work a strip more quickly as you can create the same length of row using fewer stitches and thus taking less time. However, the finished strip will look and feel slightly different to one drop (normal) Peyote.

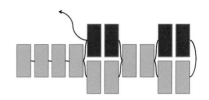

TWO DROP PEYOTE STITCH

ZIPPING UP PEYOTE STITCH

Two strips of Peyote stitch can be joined together using a technique that is referred to as 'zipping up'. The Peyote stitch edge always has a row of 'up' beads and a row of 'down' beads. If you take two strips with the same number of beads across, make sure that one strip ends with an 'up' row and the other ends with a 'down' row. Line up the edges of the strips and you should find that the two sets of beads want to dovetail together like the teeth of a zipper. Simply join them together and stitch them by passing through the first bead from the top section, the next bead from the bottom section, the next bead from the top section etc.

You can join two tubes of Peyote together in the same way. If the tubes are a square, rectangular, or hexagon shape, then make sure that the corners on each tube are precisely aligned. If this doesn't seem to be happening, then double check that the corner bead on one tube is an 'up' bead and that it is a 'down' bead on the other tube.

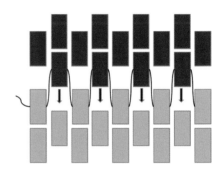

ZIPPING UP PEYOTE STITCH

TUBULAR PEYOTE STITCH

Pick up an even number of beads and string them into a circle. Tie the tail thread and working thread together to ensure that the circle is held firmly in place. This will form the first two rows of your tube.

Pick up one bead, skip a bead and pass through the next bead. Repeat this all the way around the circle until you have added half the number of beads that you used in the initial circle. At the end of the row, step up to exit from the first bead in the row you just added.

Keep repeating this pattern for as many rows as the instructions specify. You will not need to use odd count Peyote for these recipes, but it is formed in the same way, starting with an odd number of beads in the circle, so there is no step up at the end of each row - it just spirals round and round. Be careful that you do not turn even count into odd count by missing out the step up.

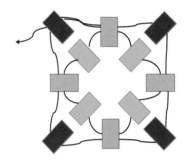

TUBULAR PEYOTE STITCH

CIRCULAR PEYOTE STITCH

Pick up the specified number of beads (usually three, four or five) and string them into a circle. Tie the tail thread and working thread together to ensure that the circle is held firmly in place. This will form the first row of your circle.

Add two beads between each of the beads in your first row. This creates the second row. Step up at the end of the row so that you exit from the first bead in the first pair of beads you added.

To make row three, add a single bead in between each bead in row two. Effectively you have just used the Peyote stitch increase in every space over these two rows to create a flat circle.

Keep adding subsequent rows by adding increases in specific places around the circle. Remember to step up at the end of each row. If you increase too often, the circle will pucker up and not lie flat. If you do not increase enough, then the circle will pull inwards instead of lying flat. If you are working on your own and not following a pattern, you may find you need to experiment to create a neat, flat circular shape with this stitch.

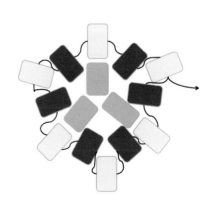

CIRCULAR PEYOTE STITCH

TRIANGULAR PEYOTE STITCH

SQUARE PEYOTE STITCH

TRIANGULAR PEYOTE STITCH

This is essentially circular Peyote, but by placing the increases in specific spaces you will make a triangle shape.

Row 1: Start with a circle of three beads.

Row 2: add two beads between each of your beads in the circle. Step up to exit from the first bead in the first pair of beads you added.

Row 3: add 2 beads and pass through the next bead in the pair. Add a single bead and pass through the first bead in the next pair. Keep adding a pair of beads between each pair from the previous row and a single bead between each of the pairs. At the end of the row, step up to exit from the first bead in the first pair of beads you added at the start of the row.

All subsequent rows are created by adding a pair of beads between each pair from the previous row (these form your corners) and stitching single beads (straight Peyote) along the sides of the triangle. Remember to step up at the end of each row.

SQUARE PEYOTE STITCH

This is another variation of circular Peyote stitch, with a different increase pattern that runs over a cycle of five rows. Each complete cycle increases by twelve beads. Remember to step up at the end of each row so that you always exit from the first bead you added at the start of that row.

Row 1: start with a circle of four beads (white in diagram).

Row 2: add a single bead between each bead in the circle (pink in diagram) – 4 beads.

Row 3: this is the start of the increase cycle. Add three beads between each bead in row 2 (brown in diagram). These will form the four corners of your square – 12 beads.

Row 4: you should have exited from the first bead in your first trio of beads. Begin this row by picking up two beads and passing through the third bead in this trio. Add 1 bead and pass through the first bead in the next trio. Add a pair of beads and pass through the third bead in the trio. Add a single bead to take you to the next trio. Repeat around the row and step up through the first bead in the first pair you added (total 12 beads). This row is shown in yellow. You should notice that you are now accentuating the corners where you are adding pairs of beads and keeping to single beads along the sides of the square.

Row 5: add a pair of beads between each of the pairs in the previous row and a single bead in each space along the sides of the square (pink in diagram) – 16 beads.

Row 6: add a single bead in between each of the beads in the previous row – this is a straight row (brown) and your shape should now look like a square – 16 beads.

Row 7: add a single bead in every space to complete your second straight row (yellow) – 16 beads. This sets you up ready to begin the next increase cycle, so you will see that you have a large space in each corner ready to add a trio of beads.

Keep repeating cycles by following the increase pattern from rows three to seven, until your square is the desired size.

I sometimes use what I refer to as a 'half increase cycle'. It is essentially the same as the cycle described above, but omits row 5 (the third row of the cycle). I use this to create a gentler edge for some of my recipes.

HEXAGON PEYOTE STITCH

Hexagon Peyote is also a form of circular Peyote with a specific increase pattern that runs over a cycle of three rows. Each complete cycle increases by six beads. Remember to step up at the end of each row so that you always exit from the first bead you added at the start of that row.

Row 1: start with a circle of three beads.

Row 2: add two beads between each of the beads in your circle (3 pairs of beads – 6 beads in total).

Row 3: add a single bead between each of the beads in the previous row (6 beads).

Row 4: this is the start of the increase cycle. Add two beads between each of the beads in row 3 (6 pairs of beads – 12 beads in total).

Row 5: add a single bead in between each bead from row 4 (total 12 beads). This completes a normal Peyote increase cycle, but is only the second row of your hexagon pattern.

Row 6: add a single bead in every space (total 12 beads). This completes the hexagon cycle.

Row 7: begin a second cycle. This will be an increase row – you will be increasing in 6 places (ie stitching a pair of beads in each of these spaces) and adding single beads in all the other spaces. The increase spaces will sit immediately above the increases you made in row 4. In stitching terms, you will add a single bead in the first space, a pair of beads in the second space, a single bead in the third space, a pair of beads in the fourth space etc. This row contains 18 beads.

Rows 8 & 9: these are straight rows to complete your second cycle, so just add one bead in every space (18 beads in each row). Row 8 confirms the increase. Row 9 sets up for the next cycle so that you can maintain the increases in the same place and thus form the corners of your hexagon.

The following row begins your third increase cycle and you should notice that you need to place the increases in the third, sixth, ninth, twelfth, fifteenth and eighteenth spaces so that they sit above the increases in row 7 and form the corners of the hexagon. The row will contain 24 beads. Complete this cycle with two more straight rows. You should now be able to understand the points at which you need to make increases and also see that the cycles are going up in multiples of 6 beads each time. The diagram shows row 6 (white) onwards. Notice how the increase spaces in row 10 (pink) sit above the increases in row 7 (pink). Keep adding cycles until you have the desired number for the pattern.

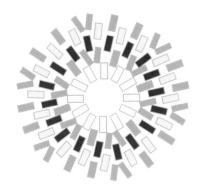

HEXAGON PEYOTE STITCH

HEXAGON CYCLE – QUICK REFERENCE

Row 1:
Increase row – add a pair of beads in each corner

. . . .

Row 2:
Straight row

. . . .

Row 3:
Straight row

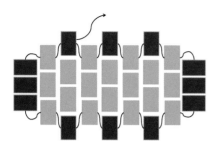

RECTANGULAR PEYOTE STITCH – BASE

RECTANGULAR PEYOTE

Rectangular Peyote starts with a strip of odd count Peyote that can be any length, but only five rows wide. The sixth row creates an end to each side of the strip so that all subsequent rows are completed in circular Peyote following either the hexagon increase pattern or the square increase pattern.

Rows 1-5: Stitch five rows of odd count straight Peyote, using the number of beads specified in the pattern.

Row 6: start stitching another row of straight Peyote, but when you get to the end of the row, instead of turning round, pick up 3 beads and pass through the end bead on the other side of your Peyote strip. Stitch along this side and add three beads at the other end. Step up to exit from the first bead you added in this row.

RECTANGULAR PEYOTE WITH HEXAGON ENDS

Stitch the first six rows as described above.

Row 7: stitch along the first side. When you reach the corner, add a pair of beads and pass through the first bead in the end trio. Add a pair of beads and pass through the third bead in the end trio. Add a pair of beads and pass through the first up bead along the second side. Stitch along the second side and add the same three pairs of beads at the other end. Step up to exit from the first bead you added at the start of the row.

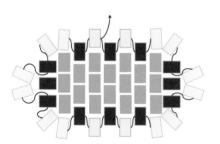

RECTANGULAR PEYOTE WITH HEXAGON ENDS

Rows 8 & 9: stitch two straight rows right around the shape, stepping up at the end of each row. This completes a hexagon cycle. For all subsequent rows, follow the hexagon increase cycle pattern, adding pairs of beads in the six corners you have established at the ends and then stitching two straight rows to maintain the pattern.

RECTANGULAR PEYOTE WITH SQUARE ENDS

Complete the first six rows to make the base of the rectangle.

Row 7: When you get to the first corner, add three beads, pass through the first bead in the end trio, add a single bead and pass through the third bead in the end trio, add three beads and pass through the first bead in the other side (yellow row in the diagram). Repeat the same increase at the other end. You should recognise this as the first step of the square increase cycle.

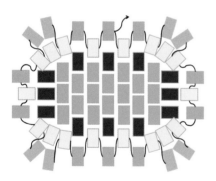

RECTANGULAR PEYOTE WITH SQUARE ENDS

Row 8: add a pair of beads in the middle of each of the trios in the four corners to continue the square increase pattern (shown in pink in the diagram).

Row 9: add a pair of beads in each corner.

Rows 10 & 11: stitch two straight rows to complete the square increase cycle.

Continue adding square cycles until your rectangle is the desired size.

LADDER STITCH

This can be done using one needle or two needles. I prefer to use one needle, so that is the method I will be describing.

Pick up two beads and pass through them again. Slide them into place so that they sit side by side with their sides touching.

Pick up a new bead and pass through the bead from which you exited and the new bead. Continue working this way and you will find that you are working in a figure of eight pattern.

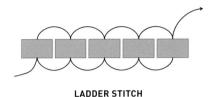

LADDER STITCH

BRICK STITCH

Stitch a foundation row of ladder stitch.

Pick up two beads and pass under the closest exposed loop of the foundation row and back up through the second bead of the two.

Pick up one bead and pass under the next exposed loop from the foundation row and back up through the bead. Continue in this way until the end of the row.

Remember to pick up two beads for the first stitch of each new row.

If you want to create tubular brick stitch, join your ladder stitch foundation into a circle by joining the first and last beads of your string in the same way that you would add a new ladder stitch bead. Then proceed with brick stitch as normal round the circle.

At the end of the row of tubular brick stitch, pass down through the first bead in the current row and back up through the next bead so that you are ready to begin a new row. Always remember to start the row by picking up two beads.

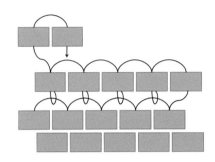

BRICK STITCH

BRICK STITCH INCREASE

To make an increase, pick up a bead and instead of passing under the next exposed loop in the previous row, pass through the same loop as the bead you just added, so you are trying to squeeze two beads into the space that would normally hold one bead.

Pick up a single bead and pass under the next exposed loop in the previous row – be very careful that you do pass under the next loop – it may be slightly obscured by your increase bead, so take care. Continue with normal brick stitch and ease the beads into place so that the increase sits comfortably in the row.

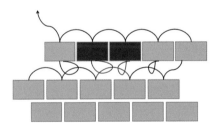

BRICK STITCH INCREASE

CHAPTER 3

USING YOUR CAKES

All of the recipes teach you how to make the basic cake, but each cake can be turned into jewellery, fridge magnets, handbag charms, key rings or just made into an ornamental gift. This chapter outlines the techniques I have used for transforming my cakes into useable items.

Birthday Cake

The 7" cake I made to celebrate the tenth anniversary of the Beadworker's Guild in 2009 started me on the beaded cakes journey.

MAKING JEWELLERY OR KEY RINGS

Some of these cakes, like the chocolate dipped strawberries, can be treated like individual beads. Rather than stringing through them (although this is possible), stitch them to one another, end to end, or include spacer beads between them to create necklaces or bracelets. Some I have stitched together to make into pendants. Some can be used singly as earrings, although you may want to think about using a small bead size so that the earrings are wearable.

Use French Wire when attaching findings or split rings

In most cases you will need to attach some kind of finding, either a clasp or an ear wire. I attached a 7mm or 9mm split ring to create a pendant finding. Make sure that the ring is large enough to allow one end of the clasp on your chosen necklace to be threaded through. When attaching any kind of finding, I prefer to use some French Wire to protect my thread from being worn as it rubs against the finding when the jewellery is being used. Key ring findings can be attached in the same way. Alternatively, attach a short length of chain with a clasp (lobster clasp or bolt clasp are best) on one end and you can create a handbag charm. The chain can be wrapped around the handle of a bag, then attach the clasp to the first ring of the chain to secure the charm in place on the bag.

If you prefer, you can add a beaded loop to act as a pendant finding through which the necklace can be threaded, or to attach a key ring.

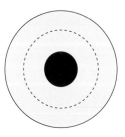

Stitch a beaded loop to use as a pendant

MAKING A FRIDGE MAGNET

Many of the projects in this book can be transformed into fridge magnets. They make a wonderfully bright display and the food theme is highly appropriate for your fridge.

Choose a magnet that has a really strong pull. The beadwork can weigh more than some shop-bought plastic fridge magnets. Some of the cake designs are also bulky, rather than flat, so they will protrude from the surface of the fridge and can be easily knocked. Therefore the stronger the pull on the magnet, the less likely they are to fall off. You can buy magnets from a lot of craft outlets. I would recommend that you avoid the very flat magnets – they tend to be weaker and they will also be more difficult to work with if you are following the instructions below. I have found an excellent source of magnets from www.first4magnets.com.

You can use strong glue and simply stick a magnet to the back of your beadwork. However, I do not recommend this method. I am always wary of trusting the glue to last over a long period of time and I also feel that putting glue onto your beads will spoil them.

Instead, I prefer to encase the magnet in a small piece of material or ribbon and then stitch this onto the beads. I feel the stitching is stronger in the long run and you can also co-ordinate your material to your beads, or to your fridge, so the result is more attractive.

FIGURE 1

Begin by cutting a circle of material about 1cm larger all round than your magnet.

Using thread to match your material, sew a running stitch in a circle slightly in from the edge of the material, but make sure that the circle is bigger than your magnet. (See figure 1).

Place your magnet in the centre of the circle of stitches and pull your thread up so that the material gathers up over the top of the magnet, encasing it completely.

Stitch the edges of the material neatly, but firmly to hold them in place on the top of the magnet. This side will look a little messy, but the other face of the magnet and its sides should be neatly covered with the material. Place the messy face against your beadwork and stitch the magnet to the beadwork, making sure that you have worked your way right around the magnet and that the unsightly edges of the material are all neatly concealed. Finish off your thread and your fridge magnet is ready to use.

Stitch the material enclosed magnet neatly to the centre of the back of your beadwork.

MAKING PLATES

A collection of cakes can be stitched onto a plate to make an ornamental gift. Plates can be made in any shape using the Peyote square, hexagon or rectangle technique. I often use size 10 beads to make my plates as they work up a little quicker than the smaller size 11 Delicas.

Flat Plate Decide on the shape that you would like and use the appropriate technique to make a flat shape. Keep stitching until your plate is large enough to hold as many cakes as you would like to display. Finish off the increase cycle and put this flat shape to one side. Make another identical flat shape, but omit the last row of the final increase cycle. Stitch the cakes onto this flat shape – this will be the top half of your plate. It is easier to stitch onto a single plate and any untidy stitching will be disguised when you join the bottom half of the plate. When all your cakes are in place, take the original flat shape and place it underneath. Align the corners and you should find that because you omitted the final row on the top half, your two flat pieces will now zip together to create a stable plate.

Raised Plate Use the same technique as above, but for the bottom half of the plate (the first one that you stitched above), add a small raised platform. When you have stitched about half the number of increase cycles you need, stitch four straight rows, then continue with the next increase cycle, making sure that you add the increases in the correct corner spaces.

Bottom view of a raised plate.

In the case of the fondant fancies, I stitched a flat hexagon until I had thirty-six beads in a row (five increase cycles) before adding the straight rows. I then stitched another five increase cycles so that I ended up with 66 beads in a row to finish the plate. The top half of the plate is simply a flat shape, in this case a flat hexagon with 66 beads in the last row and omitting the final row of this last increase cycle.

Fondant Fancies
on a raised hexagon plate

Chocolate-dipped Strawberries
on a rectangular dipping plate

Bowl or Plate with Raised Sides To make a bowl or plate with raised sides, stitch the flat shape then continue stitching straight rows to make the sides. This makes the inner (top) half of the bowl or plate. For the outer (bottom) half stitch the same flat base, but if you are making a hexagon shape, stitch an extra increase cycle before stitching up the sides. If you are making a rectangle or square bowl, then add an extra increase row (ie 2 beads in each corner) in your final increase cycle before stitching the straight rows to create the sides. You should find that the top bowl fits snugly inside the bottom bowl and you can zip up the sides along the top. Make sure that the corners are properly aligned and if you find that you are trying to stitch an 'up' row to another 'up' row rather than zipping up correctly add an extra row to one or other half so that they zip together properly.

For the chocolate dipped strawberry ornament, I made a rectangular plate using size 10 beads. I started with a string of 19 beads for rows one and two, stitched five whole increase cycles (with the extra increase row on the bottom half) and four straight rows on each half. For the chocolate pot I made an outer pot using the white beads. I stitched a flat hexagon until I had 36 beads per row in my last cycle. I then stitched twelve straight rows, ending with a 'down' bead in each corner. For the inner pot, I used chocolate coloured beads to stitch a hexagon with 30 beads per row in my final cycle. I then used white beads to stitch six straight rows, also ending with a 'down' space in each corner. I deliberately used fewer rows for the inner pot to give the impression of a bowl half filled with chocolate. When I zipped the two halves together, at each corner I passed through the two 'up' beads on either side of the corner in the outer pot and stitched them both into the 'down' space in the corner of the inner pot. This creates a sort of decrease to make sure that the two halves fit neatly. This is the only instance in which you would zip together two rows of the same type (up or down). I added the top half of a strawberry into the chocolate pot and created some strawberries without the chocolate dip.

ADDING A CAKE BOARD

Some of the full cakes are made on a cake board which is stitched as an extension of the cake itself. I then back this with card to stiffen it, using the following method.

You will need some white card – I recommend 600gsm thickness, but any that is reasonably substantial will be fine. You will also need some white felt or other similar material. It is best to use material that doesn't fray badly, so polyester jersey is a good alternative to felt.

Step 1: Draw round the base of your beaded cake board onto the white card. Cut the square/hexagon out, cutting just inside the lines you have drawn

Step 2: Take your material and cut it so that it is around 1cm (0.5") bigger than your piece of card all the way around

Step 3: Place your card in the centre of your material and cut out the corners of the material (see Fig. 1).

Step 4: Cut pieces of double sided sellotape and place one on each edge of your card. Peel off the backs and pull each edge of your material over the card and stick it down on the sellotape (see Fig.2)

Step 5: Stuff your beaded cake with white material scraps, tissue or any other suitable medium (NB it should be white) to give it a firm shape. Take your card board and, holding it wrong side up, place the beaded cake on top of it, matching the edges of the beaded base to the edges of the card base. (see Fig.3)

Step 6: Use an overstitch to stitch the cake to the board, passing through each bead and through some of the material between each bead. (see Fig.4)

To finish off, return your thread to exit from one of the beads in your final row and then add four or five straight rows of beads. You should find that these stretch down over the sides of the cake board to disguise the material and give a neat finish.

Simnel Cake
on a beaded cake board

FIGURE 1: Step 3

FIGURE 2: Step 4

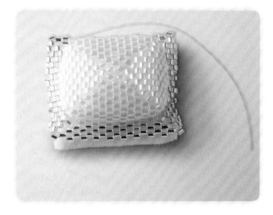

FIGURE 3: Step 5

FIGURE 4: Step 6

Recipes

Gingerbread House

My gingerbread house combines all of the ideas in this section, using different colours, different sizes, different types of beads and mixing shapes and stitches.

CHAPTER 4
MIXING BEAD COLOURS

The projects in this section are all about using colour to create distinctive foods. In each instance the shape, bead size and bead type are of one variety, created using a single stitch, but the use of particular colouring makes an instantly recognisable type of cake.

Each project is made with Peyote stitch. **The Hostess Cakes** are made using rectangular Peyote and the colour changes are relatively simple. **The Battenburg Cake** is made using square Peyote, with a mix of colours incorporated into each row. **The Swiss Roll** uses circular and tubular Peyote, but requires the careful following of a specific pattern to create the effect of the rolled cake and filling.

The Hostess with the Mostess!

page 34

Battenburg Cake

page 38

Swiss Roll

page 42

The Hostess with the Mostess!

For anyone who has visited America or who lives there, Hostess Cakes will probably be very familiar to you. An American friend, Colin, suggested these cakes to give a flavour of the USA. Twinkies are probably their best known cake, marketed as 'Golden Sponge Cake with Creamy Filling'. The recipe was invented in 1930, in Illinois, by James Alexander Dewar. He realised that several of the bakery's machines that were used to make cream-filled strawberry cake spent time un-used when strawberries were out of season. Dewar created a recipe for a snack cake filled with banana cream which would use the idle machines. He named his cake the Twinkie, claiming that the inspiration for the name came from a billboard he saw advertising 'Twinkle Toe Shoes'. During WWII bananas were rationed so the company was forced to switch to using vanilla cream instead. This proved so popular that the banana flavour was never really reintroduced until 2007, following soaring sales after promotions linked to the film King Kong.

Suzy Q's were invented in 1961. They are an oblong cake sandwich of either banana flavoured or devil's food cake, filled with white crème. The snack was named after the daughter of the Vice President of the company.

Both these recipes are made using Peyote stitch with the rectangular increase pattern. Changing bead colours represent the cream and the cake. It is the cream filling that makes the Twinkie look distinctive, so I developed a recipe to show both the whole Twinkie and also a cake cut in half to show the filling.

INGREDIENTS

Per Twinkie:
3g size 11 Delicas in DB852 for the sponge (A)
1g size 11 Delicas in DB231 for the filling (B)
Thread to match or tone with your beads

Baking time: 90 minutes

Per Suzy Q:
3g size 11 Delicas in DB734 for the chocolate sponge (C)
1g size 11 Delicas in DB231 for the filling (B)
Thread to match or tone with your beads

Baking time: 1 hour

RECIPE

Each Twinkie, whether it be a half Twinkie or a whole Twinkie, is made in two halves which are then stuffed and zipped together. The whole Twinkie uses the rectangle increase pattern with hexagon ends. The half Twinkie uses the rectangle increase pattern, but has a hexagon on one end and a half square increase on the other end. If this sounds complicated, it should all become clear below!

Half Twinkie:

Rows 1 & 2: use a stop bead to prevent your beads from slipping off the thread and leave a tail thread to be stitched in at the end. Pick up 7 (A).

Rows 3-5: stitch three rows of flat Peyote, odd count. Row 3 will contain 4 beads, row 4 will contain 3 beads and row 5 will contain 4 beads. The rows are numbered in figure 1 below.

FIGURE 1

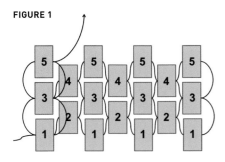

Row 6: add 3 beads along the side as if you were stitching another straight row. When you get to the end, instead of turning round, pick up 3 beads and pass through the end bead on the opposite side. Repeat down the other side and step up (12 (A) beads)

FIGURE 2

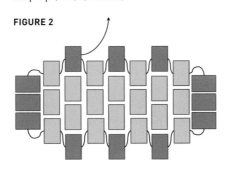

Row 7: you will now continue stitching right around your rectangle, but will add the different increase patterns for each end. Add 2 (A) along the side, then pick up 2 (A) and pass through the first bead in the group of three at the end. Pick up 2 (A) and pass through the third bead in the end group of three. Pick up 2 (A) and pass through the first up bead on the second side. This is the hexagon increase pattern. Add 2 (A) along this side, then pick up 3 (A) and pass through the first of the three beads at the end. Pick up 1(A) and pass through the third of the three end beads. Pick up 3 (A) and pass through the last bead and step up ready for the next row. This is the half

square increase (total 17 (A) beads). See figure 3.

FIGURE 3

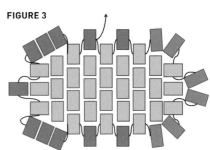

Row 8: add one (A) in each space along the sides. Add one (A) in between each of the pairs of beads on the first end (hexagon increase). When you reach the second end, pass through the first bead in the group of three, add 2 (A) and pass through the last bead in the group of three. Add an (A) in each space on the end and pass through the first bead in the group of three. Add 2 (A) and pass through the last bead in the group of three (total 17 (A) beads). See figure 4.

FIGURE 4

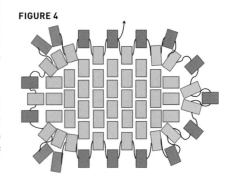

Twinkies

A key ring made with an open Twinkie and a whole Twinkie.

Row 9: add one (A) in every space. At the square increase end you will be adding one (A) between each of the pairs of beads on the corner (total 17 (A) beads).

Row 10: this is a straight row, so add one bead in every space in the following order: 11 (A), 2 (B) (these should be in the centre of the end with the square increase) and 4 (A). Step up at the end (total 15 (A), 2 (B) beads).

Row 11: stitch another straight row, but in this row you will add 3 (B) so that they sit either side of the (B) beads in your previous row – this creates the cream filling (total 14 (A), 3 (B) beads). See figure 5.

FIGURE 5

Rows 12 & 13: repeat rows 10 and 11. This completes one half, so put it to one side.

Repeat rows 1 to 12 to make the second half. Add a little bit of stuffing to each half and then join the two halves together. Align the cream filling and zip up right round the Twinkie.

Repeat this whole process to make the other part of the Twinkie. Use a square stitch to stitch the two ends of the Twinkie together along the line of cake beads next to the filling.

To make the whole Twinkie you will be following the same procedure, but your rectangle will be longer and will have the hexagon increase pattern on both ends. The entire cake will be made using (A) beads as you will not be able to see the cream filling.

Start with a string of 15 beads. Follow the same pattern as above, but when you get to row 7 add the three pairs of beads at both ends of the cake (hexagon increase cycle). In row 8, add a single bead between each pair of beads and then all subsequent rows are straight rows. Once again, make the cake in two halves, stuff each half and then zip them together. This time, make sure that you align the corners properly before you zip up.

Necklace

Necklace made with an open Twinkie, three whole Twinkies and four Suzy Qs, suspended on a chain of wave stitch.

Suzy Q

I made a single Suzy Q into a fridge magnet.

Suzy Q

The Suzy Q is also made in two halves and zipped up. The entire recipe is based on the Peyote rectangle with square increases at both ends. However, this time you will be using a full square increase cycle.

Rows 1 & 2: use a stop bead and leave a tail thread that you can stitch in later. String 11 (C).

Rows 3-5: continue with odd count straight Peyote stitch as you did for the Twinkie. Row 3 will be 6 (C), row 4 will contain 5 (C), row 5 will use 6 (C).

Row 6: add a single (C) bead in each space along the side, add 3 (C) at each end (total 16 (C) beads).

Row 7: add a single (C) in each space along the sides. When you reach the corner, add 3 (C), pass through the first in the group of three from the previous row, add 1 (C) and pass through the last bead in the group of three from the previous row, add 3 (C). Remember to step up at the end of the row (total 22 (C) beads).

Row 8: add a single (C) in each space along the side. When you reach the groups of three beads at each corner, pass through the first bead in the group, pick up two (C) and pass through the last bead in the group. Continue adding single beads and step up at the end of the row (total 22 (C) beads).

Row 9: add a single (C) in each space and 2 (C) in between each pair of beads at the corner (total 26 (C) beads).

Rows 10 & 11: these are both straight rows, so add a single (C) in each space and step up at the end of each row (total 26 (C) beads).

Rows 12 & 13: these are both straight rows. You will find that the sides of the cake start to form (total 26 (C) beads).

Row 14: this is a decrease row so that the sponge is pulled in to create a distinction between the cake and the filling. When you reach the corner, pass through two beads to make a decrease. Repeat this at every corner (total 22 (C) beads). See figure 6.

FIGURE 6

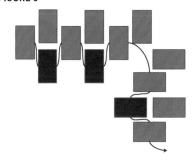

Row 15: stitch a straight row to complete the decrease (total 22 (C) beads).

Rows 16 & 17: stitch two straight rows using the (B) beads to form your filling (total 22 (B) beads per row). This completes the first half of your Suzy Q, so put it to one side.

Make the second half by repeating rows 1 to 16 (note you will only have 1 row of filling on this half). Align the two halves so that the corners are correctly matched and then zip up the cake. This cake should not need stuffing.

This completes your Suzy Q.

Battenburg Cake

Battenburg cake was created in 1884 in honour of the marriage of Queen Victoria's granddaughter to Prince Louis of Battenburg. The cake is a four square check pattern made from two different coloured rectangles of sponge cake, glued together with jam and covered in marzipan. The squares were designed to represent the four princes of Battenburg, Alexander, Louis, Henry and Francis-Joseph.

To make the real cake, you would need to make a sponge mixture, divide it in two and dye one half pink and the other half yellow. Cook the two sponges in a rectangular baking tin. When they are cooked and have cooled, cut each sponge in half lengthways so that their profiles form the squares. Roll out the marzipan and arrange the sponge pieces on the marzipan, gluing them together with apricot jam. Spread more apricot jam on the top and sides of the sponge and wrap the marzipan round to encase the cake. Thankfully, the beaded version is a lot simpler to make! This is simply a Peyote square in which you will combine different bead colours to make the distinctive pattern that forms this cake. If you are new to the three-dimensional beading in this book, then this recipe is a great place to start. Make sure you have familiarised yourself with the Peyote stitch square increase cycle and you are ready to go. I had a lot of fun designing different jewellery with this pattern, or just make the straightforward cake. It is a joy to work with this combination of coloured beads, so have fun and see where your imagination takes you!

INGREDIENTS

Per cake:
1g size 11 Delicas in DB709 for the jam (A)
3g size 11 Delicas in DB625 for the pink sponge (B)
3g size 11 Delicas in DB751 for the yellow sponge (C)
9g size 11 Delicas in DB232 for the marzipan (D)
15g size 10 Delicas in DB201 to make the plate
Thread to match or tone with your beads

Baking time:
4 hours for the cake, 90 minutes for the slice

RECIPE

I thought it would be rather fun to make a cake with a slice cut from it, sitting on a plate. This reduces the stitching time for the cake since there is no need to make it as long as a complete cake would appear. The cake is made using the circular Peyote stitch with the square increase cycle to make a flat square. You will then continue stitching tubular Peyote stitch to create the sides of the cake. You will make two identical halves in this manner and then zip them up to join them together at the end. The slice is made as a square using the same pattern, then adding the sides. It is stitched straight to the plate to save making a bottom side for it.

Row 1: pick up 4 (A) and tie them into a circle, leaving a tail thread that you can stitch in later. Pass through the first two beads again.

Row 2: add 1 (A) between each of the beads in your circle (total 4 (A) beads).

Row 3: add 3 (B) in the first space, 3 (C) in the second space, 3 (B) in the third space and 3 (C) in the fourth space. Step up through the first (B) in your first group of three (total 6 (B), 6 (C) beads). See figure 1.

FIGURE 1

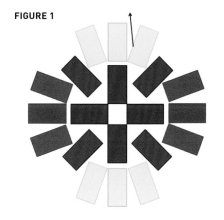

Row 4: follow the square increase cycle and add a pair of (B), 1 (A), a pair of (C), 1 (A), a pair of (B), 1 (A), a pair of (C), 1 (A) and step up through the first (B) added (total 4 (A), 4 (B), 4 (C) beads). See figure 2.

FIGURE 2

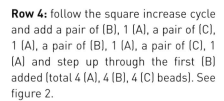

Row 5: add a pair of (B), 1 (B), 1 (C), a pair of (C), 1 (C), 1 (B). Repeat this sequence and step up through the first (B) added (total 8 (B), 8 (C) beads). See figure 3.

FIGURE 3

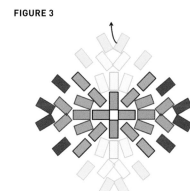

Row 6: this is the first straight row in your first increase cycle. You should notice that the pattern of sponge squares and jam is clearly forming now. In this row you will add 4 (A) beads to maintain the jam pattern, but notice that you only add (A) beads in each alternate row. Total 4 (A), 6 (B) and 6 (C) beads. See figure 4.

FIGURE 4

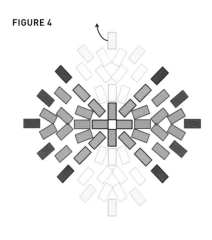

FIGURE 5

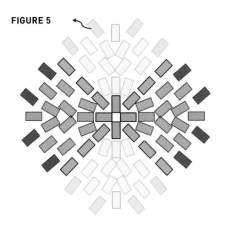

Row 7: this is also a straight row and it completes your first increase cycle. In this row you will not be adding any (A) beads, just maintain the pattern adding the (B) and (C) beads in the correct quadrants. Remember to step up at the end of the row. Total 8 (B) and 8 (C) beads. See figure 5.

You are now ready to begin the next increase cycle.

Row 8: add three beads in each corner, maintain the pattern you have established and remember to step up at the end of the row. Total 4 (A), 10 (B), 10 (C).

Row 9: add a pair of beads in the centre of the triple set in each corner. Total 12 (B), 12 (C).

Row 10: add a pair of beads in each corner. Total 4 (A), 12 (B), 12 (C).

Row 11: this is a straight row. Total 14 (B), 14 (C).

Row 12: this is another straight row. Total 4 (A), 12 (B), 12 (C).

Row 13: this is the start of your third and final increase cycle. Add 3 beads in each corner space. Total 18 (B), 18 (C).

Row 14: continue the cycle by adding a pair of beads in each corner. Total 4 (A), 16 (B), 16 (C).

Row 15: add a pair of beads in each corner in this row. Total 20 (B), 20 (C).

Row 16: this is a straight row and in this row you will start adding the marzipan coating, so stitch the entire row using the (D) beads. Total 40 (D).

Row 17: this completes your final increase cycle. It is another straight row and is also stitched entirely in (D) beads. Total 40 (D).

Rows 18-32: these are all straight rows, stitched with the (D) beads. You will find the square starts to turn into a tube to make the sides of your cake. Total 40 (D) in each row.

Put the first half of your cake to one side. Make a second half in exactly the same way, stitching rows 1 to 31. Add a little bit of stuffing to each half. Place the two halves together, match up the corners and zip the edges together to finish off your cake. Also make sure that you match up the coloured squares in the two halves so that the cake continues from front to back.

Battenburg Slice

The slice is made by stitching rows 1 to 23. You may want to add a bit of stuffing to the slice when you stitch it onto the plate.

The plate is made with size 10 Delicas. Use the rectangular increase method, starting with 19 beads in the first two rows and completing 4 cycles. When you have completed the first three rows of your final increase cycle, stitch the cake and slice onto the plate. Make sure that you line up to colours so that it appears that the slice has been cut from the cake. Then add a card backing and finish off the plate. See page 29 for full instructions.

Battenburg Earrings

I made the earrings using size 15 beads and just two increase cycles, ie rows 1 to 12. Remember that rows 11 and 12 will use all (D) beads to add the marzipan. Add two straight rows of marzipan to complete one half. For the second half, just add a single straight row of marzipan. Add a bit of stuffing and zip up the two halves.

Battenburg Pendant

The components of the pendant were made using size 11 beads. The larger slice follows all three increase cycles, one half adding a single straight row and the other half adding two straight rows, as for the earrings. The smaller slice is made with just two increase cycles but with the same number of straight rows as the larger slice. Join the corners of the slices together. I added a necklace to this pendant and created a dual fastening using two magnetic clasps where the necklace beads join the slices of Battenburg.

Dual fastening using two magnetic clasps where the necklace beads join the slices of Battenburg

You can use any kind of clasp you like, but ensure that the two sides look as though they match. This way the clasp becomes a feature of the design. I used a combination of pink and yellow beads from my existing bead stash, just choosing colours that brought out the colouring of the Battenburg slices.

The bracelet is made in two halves: top and bottom. Each half is a series of squares joined together. Make the first square using two increase cycles, as for the earrings, remembering to stitch rows 11 and 12 with (D) beads.

For the second square, stitch rows 1 to 10, but as you start row 11 you will be joining this square onto the first square, corner to corner. Make sure you line up the colours so that a pink corner on the second square joins a yellow corner on the first square.

Row 11: begin stitching the straight row with (D) beads. When you reach the pink corner, instead of passing through the corner pair, pass through the bead on the right hand side of the corner on the first square. Then pass through the pair of beads on the second square. Pass through the bead on the left of the corner of the first square, pick up a (D) and pass through the next bead on the second square. The thread path is shown in figure 6.

Row 12: add a straight row using (D) beads. When you reach the corner join, pass through the row 11 bead that joins onto square 1 (shown in orange). Pick up a (D) (shown in green) and pass through the corner bead in the first square, then the pair of beads in the second square and the other corner bead in the first square, following the same thread path as you did in row 11. Pick up another (D), also shown in green and then through the equivalent bead in square 2 (shown in orange). See figure 7 for the thread path. You should find that this is more obvious as you work than it sounds when described! The aim is to create a neat join that maintains the square Peyote shape, so as long as you achieve this, the method you use is up to you!

FIGURE 6

FIGURE 7

Keep making and adding squares until your bracelet is the desired length.

Stitch a straight row of (D) beads right around the outside of the entire bracelet. When you reach an outer corner you will be adding a single bead in the space so the beads will start to curl down into the beginnings of a tube. Each time you reach a corner joining two squares, pass through two beads to form a decrease. You will find that the beads naturally want to make this decrease.

Make another identical bracelet strip, but do not add the straight row round the outside. Instead match the two halves of the bracelet to one another (if you are having trouble with this, make sure that the corner beads align and the rest will naturally follow) and zip up the two halves. Finally add a clasp of your choice to complete the bracelet. I added a button clasp underneath the bracelet so that the two ends would meet and the clasp would not be visible. A magnetic clasp would also work.

Battenburg Bracelet

Swiss Roll

The origins of this popular cake are rather unclear. I believe the recipe originated in central Europe, but apparently not in Switzerland, so why it is known as a 'Swiss' roll is a mystery! It is also known as a Roulade. It is basically a thin rectangle of sponge that is spread with a filling – traditionally jam – and then rolled up. Viewed end on, this gives a distinctive spiral of jam and sponge. The jam can be replaced with cream or chocolate and the cake can also be made as a plain sponge or a chocolate sponge. In the US and the UK, this tea-time cake has been adapted to form the basis of the Christmas Yule Log. Chocolate sponge is mixed with cream or vanilla icing and then the entire roll can be covered in chocolate icing and decorated with icing sugar and a sprig of edible holly.

I decided to make this recipe as it looks so distinctive in both its vanilla and chocolate forms. This is the perfect example of the way in which simply using different coloured beads in a particular pattern can create an immediately recognisable cake. This pattern uses hexagonal Peyote stitch and a carefully calculated arrangement of beads to create the spiral effect. It is a good exercise in following a pattern.

INGREDIENTS

Per Slice:
4g size 11 Delicas in DB852 for the sponge (A)
1g size 11 Delicas in DB295 for the jam (B)
Thread to match or tone with your beads

Baking time: 1 hour

RECIPE

Each slice of swiss roll is made in two halves and then zipped up at the end. Both halves are made using circular Peyote stitch and employing the hexagon increase pattern. Make sure that you are really familiar with this stitch before you start trying to follow this pattern. I have listed the exact order in which you will pick up the different coloured beads in each row, but I have not specified the points at which you will be making increases as I am assuming prior knowledge of that.

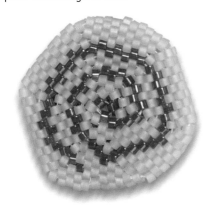

Detail of the Swiss Roll pattern

The photo shows a detail of the face of the swiss roll, so consult that as you are working if you are unsure about the pattern.

Row 1: working with a comfortable length of thread, pick up 3 (B) beads. Leaving a tail thread that you can stitch in at the end, tie the two ends of your thread together so that your beads form a circle.

Row 2: is an increase row in which you will add 1 (B), 5 (A) and step up at the end of the row (total 6 beads).

Row 3: add 1 (B), 5 (A) and step up at the end of the row (total 6 beads).

Row 4: is an increase row, so add 1 (B) and 11 (A) and step up at the end of the row (total 12 beads).

Row 5: add 9 (B) and 3 (A) and step up at the end of the row (total 12 beads).

Row 6: add 9 (B) and 3 (A) and step up at the end (total 12 beads).

Row 7: is an increase row, so add 12 (A), 3 (B), 3 (A) and step up at the end of the row (total 18 beads).

Row 8: add 12(A), 1 (B), 1(A), 1(B), 3(A) and step up at the end of the row (total 18 beads).

Row 9: add 14(A), 1(B), 3(A) and step up at the end of the row (total 18 beads).

Row 10: is an increase row in which you will add 10(B), 2(A), 2(B), 5(A), 5(B) and step up (total 24 beads).

Row 11: add 1(A), 3(B), 1(A), 3(B), 1(A), 3(B), 1(A), 1(B), 5(A), 1(B), 1(A), 3(B) and step up (total 24 beads).

Row 12: add 9 (A), 2 (B), 13 (A) and step up (total 24 beads). From this point on you will be finishing off the cake, so adding no more jam beads.

Row 13: a real swiss roll has an uneven base where the end of the rolled cake sits, so this row starts to create that uneven shape by omitting a few spaces part way through the row. This is an increase row, but you will end up missing one of the increases, so the total bead count is not what you would expect.

Add 16 (A), skip the next 3 spaces (see figure 1), add 10 (A) and step up (total 27 beads).

FIGURE 1

Row 14: again, this row misses some spaces to maintain the shaped edge of the cake. Add 16 (A), but as you add the last bead you will need to pass back through the bead below and then weave your thread back in the original direction of travel and skip the next 3 spaces (see figure 2). Continue with the rest of the row as normal, adding 10(A) and stepping up (total 26 beads).

FIGURE 2

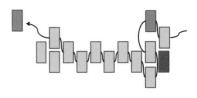

Row 15: add 29(A), so work your way right around the entire row adding a bead in each space. This involves a small section of slightly free-form Peyote in the area where you have missed the beads in rows 13 and 14 (see figure 3). When you reach the gap, pick up 1 bead and pass through the next 'up' bead (also the next but one bead). This will take your bead level down slightly, so your work may begin to pull in a little, but don't worry. Pick up another bead and pass through the next but one bead

(this will be the next 'up' bead). Pick up another bead and pass through the next 'up' bead. You will notice that these beads are in a diagonal (highlighted in yellow in figure 3). Pick up a fourth bead and pass through the third bead in the diagonal. You should now be back to the normal stitching area, so continue as usual. Step up at the end of the row (total 29 beads).

FIGURE 3

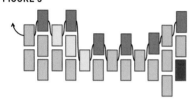

Rows 16-18: these are all straight rows in which you will add 29(A) – one bead in each space – and step up at the end of each row. These form the sides of the swiss roll slice (total 29 beads per row).

Leave your working thread as you may need to use it to zip up the two halves and put this finished half to one side.

Make a second half following exactly the same pattern, but omit row 18. In order to make sure that the swirl of jam matches as if it continued right the way through the slice, you will need the pattern on your two halves to be a mirror image on each. As you are stitching the straight rows, you will find that your beadwork naturally starts to curl towards you to form a tube. Allow this to happen on your first half, but on the second half, encourage the beadwork to curl back away from you. That way the two halves will naturally mirror one another.

Put the two halves together and zip them up. As you do so, be very careful to align them correctly – make sure that the free-form areas on both halves are in exactly the same place and that the corner sections on each half also align. Finish off any tail threads and your slice of Swiss Roll is finished.

Swiss Roll Slice Pendant
I made a smaller slice using size 15 beads and paired it with a normal slice to create a pendant.

If you would like to make a chocolate Swiss Roll, then use DB709 for your (A) beads and DB231 for your (B) beads.

For the whole Swiss roll, stitch an additional 17 straight rows on each half, so each row will contain 29(A) beads. I put this on a plate made using rectangular Peyote increase pattern. Start with 13 size 10 Delicas for your first two rows. Complete two increase cycles. Stitch the first two rows of the third increase cycle, then add a cake board backing (see page 29) and stitch a further 5 rows of straight Peyote.

I made the Yule Log by making a chocolate swiss roll covered in a layer of chocolate icing and decorated with icing sugar and a piece of holly. As the roll is covered in chocolate, the ends will lose their distinctive swirl of icing. I overcame this problem by constructing a Yule Log on a plate with a slice cut from it, also lying on the plate. Make the slice as normal, but use DB0734 for rows 15 onwards and instead of making two sides to the slice, add two extra rows (total 20 rows) and then stitch it directly onto your choice of plate. The large log is made in two halves.

For the first half, follow the pattern for the slice, again using DB0734 for rows 15 onwards and stitch 30 rows in total. For the second half, use DB0734 for the entire shape and stitch a total of 29 rows. Make sure that the end representing the inside of the cake is stitched to the plate next to the cut slice. Take care that you line up the swirl of cream on both the slice and the whole cake so that it looks as if the slice has been cut from the log and left on the plate. For this plate, I started with 17 size 10 Delicas for the first two rows. Complete two increase cycles, then stitch the first two rows of the third increase cycle. Add the card and felt backing and then continue stitching a further 5 straight rows to bring the cakeboard down over the sides. Add the icing sugar to the top of the main log using the method outlined in the Victoria Sponge recipe. I then made a piece of holly on one end as follows:

Step 1: exit from an icing bead and pick up 7 size 11 green Delica beads.

Step 2: pass your needle through the fourth bead you just picked up (see figure 4).

FIGURE 4

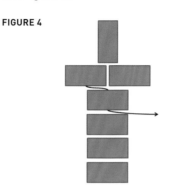

Step 3: pick up 1 size 11 green Delica and pass through the next but one bead in your strip. Pick up 1 size 11 green Delica and pass through the icing bead from which you first started. This completes your first holly leaf (see figure 5).

FIGURE 5

Step 4: repeat steps 1 to 3 to make a second leaf. This will naturally sit opposite the first leaf.

Step 5: add a cluster of size 11 red Delicas between your two leaves to make the berries.

Step 6: finally, add a third leaf and encourage this to sit at right angles to the first two leaves. Your holly sprig is complete. You can add extra leaves or add extra sprigs along the log as you wish.

Yule Log

CHAPTER 5

MIXING BEAD SIZES

All the projects in this section use a mixture of different sized beads of the same type in order to create a particular object or effect. Whilst colours may change, it is this mixture of sizing that creates the desired effect for each of these sweet treats.

Each of these projects uses Peyote stitch. **The Victoria Sponge** uses circular and tubular Peyote, but relies on different sized beads to create the effect of jam in the centre and icing sugar on the top. **The Chocolate Dipped Strawberries** also use circular and tubular Peyote and rely on mixing bead size to create the effect of chocolate coating on each strawberry. **The chocolate eclairs** are made using rectangular and tubular Peyote. Varying bead sizes create the effect of chocolate on top and give the texture of the cream in the centre. **The donuts** are made using circular and tubular Peyote and it is only by mixing bead sizes that the donut shape can be created.

Victoria Sponge   page 48

Chocolate Dipped Strawberries   page 52

Chocolate Eclairs   page 56

Donuts   page 60

Victoria Sponge

The Victoria Sponge is a very traditional British tea-time treat. I do not know who first invented this recipe, but it gained its name in the reign of Queen Victoria. Apparently she enjoyed a slice of this cake with her afternoon tea. It is a traditional vanilla sponge cake that is baked, then sliced in half. The two halves are sandwiched back together with a layer of jam (and possibly also cream) and then icing sugar is sprinkled on the top.

Sophy suggested this recipe to me. It is both very distinctive and beautifully traditional. For anyone who has already read my first book of miniature beaded occasion cakes, this recipe will be completely familiar. It uses the hexagon Peyote pattern to create a flat circular top and then uses straight Peyote stitch to create the sides. I wanted to find a way to incorporate the layer of jam into the cake and make it look as though it had a different texture from the sponge sides of the cake. I did this by mixing my bead sizes. The sponge is made with size 10 delicas, the jam with size 11 delicas. The smaller bead size allowed me to stitch 2 beads in every space so that the beads gathered up slightly and gave the impression of jam just seeping out from between the layers of sponge. I topped the cake off with a scattering of size 15 delicas to represent the icing sugar. I also developed this idea to make a single slice, which makes a great key ring, handbag charm or even fridge magnet. So, have some fun here and this is for Sophy with thanks for a really great idea!

INGREDIENTS

Per Cake:
25g size 10 Delicas in DB852 for the sponge (A)
2g size 11 Delicas in DB295 for the jam (B)
1g size 15 beads in Ceylon white for the icing sugar (C)
10g size 10 Delicas in DB201 for the plate (D)
Thread to match or tone with your beads

Baking time: 8 hours

RECIPE

This cake is made with a flat Peyote stitch hexagon for the top, continuing into straight Peyote stitch to make the sides. The jam is added as you stitch and you can add the icing sugar before or after adding the plate. The plate is made by following the instructions for a cakeboard.

Make a flat Peyote stitch hexagon, continuing to stitch until you have 60 beads in a row and have completed the final increase cycle. Make sure that you are familiar with the hexagon increase pattern before you begin this project. The bead count in each row will be as follows:

Row 1: 3 (A) beads

Row 2: 6 (A) beads – this is an increase row

Row 3: 6 (A) beads

Row 4: 12 (A) beads – this is an increase row

Rows 5 & 6: 12 (A) beads

Row 7: 18 (A) beads – this is an increase row

Rows 8 & 9: 18 (A) beads

Row 10: 24 (A) beads - this is an increase row

Rows 11 & 12: 24 (A) beads

Row 13: 30 (A) beads – this is an increase row

Rows 14 & 15: 30 (A) beads

Row 16: 36 (A) beads – this is an increase row

Rows 17 & 18: 36 (A) beads

Row 19: 42 (A) beads – this is an increase row

Rows 20 & 21: 42 (A) beads

Row 22: 48 (A) beads – this is an increase row

Rows 23 & 24: 48 (A) beads

Row 25: 54 (A) beads – this is an increase row

Rows 26 & 27: 54 (A) beads

Row 28: 60 (A) beads – this is an increase row

Rows 29 & 30: 60 (A) beads – this completes your final cycle

Rows 31-38: 60 (A) beads

Rows 39 & 40: add 2 (B) beads in every space. Your beadwork will start to wrinkle up, but it should gradually straighten out again as you return to straight rows of sponge.

Jam up close.

Rows 41-48: 60 (A) beads

You can either continue on and add the cake board at this stage, or first add the icing sugar for the top and then come back to the cake board. The cake board bead count is as follows:

Row 49: 66 (D) beads – this is an increase row

Row 50 & 51: 66 (D) beads

Row 52: 72 (D) beads – this is an increase row

Rows 52 & 53: 72 (D) beads

Row 54: 78 (D) beads – this is an increase row

Row 55: 78 (D) beads

Add the card and felt backing, following the instructions on page 29.

Rows 56-60: 78 (D) beads to take the beads down over the edges of the cake board and give it a good finish.

Icing sugar up close.

The icing sugar is added using the (C) beads. Thread a new length of thread, starting in the centre top of the cake, exit from a sponge bead, pick up 1(C) and pass through a sponge bead next to the one from which you exited. Pass through a sponge bead, or two and exit. Repeat the whole process over and over until you have added icing sugar as if it were sprinkled across the top of the cake. Don't add it too close to the edges and make sure that it is more concentrated near the centre and a little more thinly spread towards the cake edges to try and create a little realism. Your Victoria sponge is now finished.

Victoria Sponge Slice

I made the slice of Victoria Sponge by following basically the same recipe. However, I used a triangle shape instead of the hexagon, so first familiarise yourself with the triangle increase pattern. I also made the cake in two halves as I decided not to stitch it onto a plate.

To make the top half, follow the triangular increase pattern until you have 30 beads in a row.

Your bead count will be as follows:

Row 1: 3 (A) beads

Row 2: 6 (A) beads

Row 3: 9 (A) beads

Row 4: 12 (A) beads

Row 5: 15 (A) beads

Row 6: 18 (A) beads

Row 7: 21 (A) beads

Row 8: 24 (A) beads

Row 9: 27 (A) beads

Row 10: 30 (A) beads

Continue following rows 31 to 41 from the main cake recipe. Add the icing sugar to the top of this half and then put it to one side.

To make the bottom half, follow the pattern of rows 1 to 10 laid out above. Add 8 straight rows and then join the two halves together. Before joining them, add some stuffing to help the slice to hold its shape. First make sure that you have aligned all the corners correctly and then zip up to complete your slice.

Victoria Sponge Key Ring
A slice of Victoria Sponge made into a key ring

Chocolate Dipped Strawberries

Nobody is quite sure where or when chocolate dipped strawberries first appeared. Some stories claim that they were created by Lorraine Lorusso during the 1960s and first sold at a store called 'Stop n Shop' in Chicago, Illinois. Other sources claim that they originated in Italy.

They may also be linked to the appearance of the chocolate fondue. This originated in a New York restaurant called 'Chalet Suisse' in 1966. The restaurant owner, a Swiss-born immigrant called Konrad Egli, invented the fondue as a marketing gimmick to launch Toblerone in the USA. Traditionally all manner of fruits are served alongside the fondue to be dipped in the warm melted chocolate and eaten.

Whatever the origins of this delicious treat, I designed my beaded version after receiving the suggestion from Johannes. The shape and colour make these little treats very distinctive. I found that mixing bead sizes enabled me to give the illusion that the layer of chocolate was coating the strawberry, rather than that I had simply decided to change bead colour halfway through making my fruit. This recipe uses circular Peyote stitch and, by increasing and decreasing in the right spaces, the distinctive strawberry shape is created. Dedicated to the lovely beaders I met in Cornwall where I was privileged to teach my very first workshop – thank you!

INGREDIENTS

1g size 11 seed beads in your choice of green (A)
1g size 11 delicas DB295 (B)
1g size 10 delicas DB715 (C)
Thread to match or tone with your beads

Baking time: 30 minutes

Make a loop of beads to act
as a Pendant finding.

RECIPE

Each strawberry is made using circular Peyote stitch. You may wish to use green thread to make the leaves and then start a new red thread for the strawberry, or you can use a single length of thread that will tone with all the beads, eg Crystal Fireline.

Begin by making the leaves.

Row 1: Pick up 3 (A) and, leaving a tail long enough to stitch in and finish off at the end, pass through all the beads again so that they form a circle.

Row 2: Pick up 2 (A) and pass through the next bead in row 1. Repeat twice more to complete the row (this is an increase row with a total of 6 beads in it). Step up by passing your needle through the first bead in row 2.

Row 3: Add 1 (A) between each of the beads in row 2 and remember to step up at the end of the row (total 6 (A) beads).

Row 4: Add 2 (A) between each of the beads in row 3 (ie this is an increase row). Step up at the end of the row by passing through the first of the beads that you have just added, so you will exit in the middle of a group of 2 beads (total 12(A) beads).

Row 5: Pick up 1 (A) and pass through the second bead in the pair. Pass through the adjacent bead from row 3 and exit from the first bead in your next group of 2. Repeat all the way round the row. This creates the shape of the leaves. You are adding 1 (A) in between each pair of beads and missing the space between the pairs (total 6 (A) beads). See figure 1.

FIGURE 1

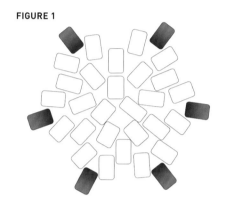

If you are planning to attach a pendant or key ring, then pass your needle back through the leaves until it exits from a bead in row 1. Pick up 1 bead and pass through the next bead in row 1. *Pick up 1 bead and pass through the bead you just added. Repeat from * until you have added 16 beads in total. See figure 2.

FIGURE 2

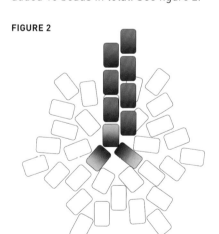

To make the strawberry into a pendant, join this string of beads back onto the leaves by taking the end back to the leaves to form a loop. Pass through a bead in the first row of the leaves and then pass back through the last bead added to the loop. Make sure this is securely stitched in place and finish off all your threads.

If you are adding a key ring, thread the string of beads through the key ring finding before stitching the end of it to the leaves to form the loop.

If you are making earrings, instead of stitching a loop of beads, add a split ring in the centre of the leaves and finish off your thread securely. You can then use the split ring to attach the earring findings.

Strawberry

Now add the strawberry to the leaves. Either join a new thread or take your existing thread to exit from a leaf bead in the second row of your leaves (shown in green in figure 3). You will be working in circular Peyote as follows:

Row 1: pick up 1 (B) and pass through the next leaf bead. Repeat all the way round the row. Step up at the end of the row to exit from the first red bead you added. Figure 3 indicates in white the leaf beads that are behind the red rows you are adding (total 6 (B) beads).

FIGURE 3

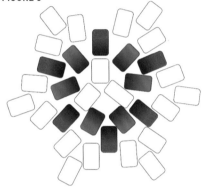

Row 2: add 2 (B) between each of the beads in row 1 – this is an increase row (total 12 (B) beads).

Rows 3 – 8: stitch 6 straight rows using the (B) beads. Keep your tension tight and the rows will start to take on a tubular shape, making the sides of the strawberry (total 12 (B) beads per row).

Row 9: stitch another straight row, but start adding chocolate beads. Pick up 1 (C), 1 (B), 1 (C), 1 (B), 1 (C), 1 (B), 4 (C), 2 (B) and step up (total 5 (B), 7 (C) beads).

Row 10: stitch a straight row with 5 (C), 1 (B), 5 (C), 1 (B) and step up (total 2 (B), 10 (C) beads).

Rows 11 & 12: stitch 2 straight rows using all (C) beads (total 12 (C) beads per row).

Row 13: This is your first decrease row. Pick up 1 (C) and pass through the next bead in the previous row, pick up 1 (C) and pass through the next bead in the previous row, pick up 1 (C) and pass through the next two beads in the previous row to make a decrease. Repeat this sequence twice more to complete the row (total 9 (C) beads).

Rows 14 & 15: Stitch two straight rows of (C) beads. Step up at the end of each row (total 9 (C) beads).

Row 16: This is the second decrease row. Pick up 1 (C) and pass through the next two beads in the previous row. Pick up 1 (C) and pass through the next single bead in the previous row. Repeat this sequence twice more to complete the row. Notice that the place in which each decrease sits is directly above the decreases you made in row 13.

You should find that the bottom of the strawberry starts to form a pyramid shape with three clear sides leading down to the pointed tip. Figure 4 shows the decrease pattern as if viewed from one side – each bead contains its row number (total 6 (C) beads).

Rows 17 & 18: Stitch two straight rows of (C) beads. Step up at the end of each row (total 6 (C) beads per row).

FIGURE 4

Row 19: This is the final decrease row. Pick up 1 (C) and pass through the next two beads in the previous row. Repeat twice more to complete the row (total 3 (C) beads).

Row 20: stitch a straight row of (C) beads to finish off the strawberry. Finish your thread securely. If you are making a pendant, key ring or fridge magnet, you will need to make more strawberries, but do not add a loop to the leaves. Stitch all your strawberries together in your desired arrangement, making sure that the strawberry with the key ring attachment or pendant loop is at the top of the arrangement.

Strawberry Fridge Magnet

I used 5 strawberries to make a fridge magnet and arranged them so that I could stitch the magnet to the centre of the group and it would not be visible from the front.

Strawberry Key Ring
I paired a normal sized strawberry with a larger version,
both with striped chocolate, to make a key ring.

If you want to make a larger strawberry, follow exactly the same process, but add some extra rows as follows:

For the leaves, stitch rows **1 to 4** as outlined above.

Rows 5 & 6: stitch two more straight rows (total 12 beads per row).

Row 7: add 2 beads, then skip a bead: pass through the next bead from row 6, down through the bead in row 5 and up through the following bead in row 6. Repeat 5 more times to complete the row (total 12 beads).

Row 8: Add 1 bead between each of the pairs of beads you added in row 7 (total 6 beads). This completes the leaves, so either finish off your thread or add a loop for a pendant or key ring.

For the strawberry, stitch rows 1 to 4 as outlined above.

Row 5: increase to 18 beads per row – add 2 (B) in the first space, 1 (B) in the next space and so on round the row to complete the increase row.

Rows 6-11: stitch straight rows using all red beads (total 18 (B) beads per row).

Rows 12-15: stitch straight rows, but gradually add the chocolate beads (total 18 bead per row – mix (B) and (C) beads).

Row 16: this is a decrease row using all (C) beads. Decrease on the 3rd, 8th and 13th spaces so that you have 15 beads in a row.

Rows: 17, 18: stitch two straight rows in (C) beads (total 15 (C) beads per row).

Row 19: this is the second decrease row. Decrease on the 1st, 5th and 9th spaces so that you have twelve beads in a row.

Rows 20 & 21: stitch two straight rows in (C) beads (total 12 (C) beads per row).

Rows 22 to end: as for rows 13-20 in the small strawberry. Make sure that all your decreases line up as they did for the small strawberry.

To add spiralling white chocolate stripes to your chocolate dip, use size 10 Delicas in Ceylon White (DB0201). For the first row of chocolate beads (row 9 for the smaller strawberry), add 2 brown beads and 1 white bead all the way around the row. Maintain this order of beads for all subsequent rows and you will see the stripes spiral round the strawberry. In decrease rows you may need to cheat a little on the order of beads so that you maintain the effect of the stripes as closely as possible.

Chocolate Eclairs

Chocolate Eclairs originated in late nineteenth-century France and the recipe is often attributed to the famous chef Marie-Antoine Careme. However the first written recipe was recorded in the Boston School Cooking Book by Mrs D. A. Lincoln in 1884.

This delicious dessert is traditionally an oblong of choux pastry filled with cream and topped with chocolate icing. The authentic recipe for choux pastry makes a pastry with a hollow centre, created as it bakes. The cream should then be piped into this hollow when the pastry has cooled. Some variations use a slightly different pastry recipe, then slice the resulting pastry in half, fill the two halves with cream and add the chocolate icing.

I used both ideas for inspiration and created two slightly different variations of chocolate éclair. In both cases I used different sized beads to give the appearance of the chocolate icing sitting on top of the pastry. In one variation I made the traditional version with the cream in the centre, not visible from the outside. For the other variation I used different sized beads to create a strip of cream and placed it between the two halves. This recipe is all about mixing bead sizes to create different effects. I made this recipe for my Mum, with lots of love!

INGREDIENTS

Per Éclair with cream:
2g size 10 Delicas in DB715 for the chocolate (A)
5g size 11 Delicas in DB852 for the pastry (B)
120 size 15 white or cream seed beads (C)
60 size 11 white or cream seed beads (D)
30 size 8 white or cream seed beads (E)
Thread to match or tone with your beads

Baking time: 2 hours

Per traditional eclair:
2g size 10 Delicas in DB715 for the chocolate (A)
6g size 11 Delicas in DB852 for the pastry (B)
Thread to match or tone with your beads

Baking time: 1 hour

RECIPE

Each part of the eclair is made in two halves which are then stuffed and zipped together. The recipe uses the rectangle increase pattern with hexagon ends. The cream is made with tubular Peyote stitch.

Top half of the eclair:

Rows 1 & 2: use a stop bead to prevent your beads from slipping off the thread and leave a tail thread to be stitched in at the end. Pick up 13 (A).

Rows 3-5: stitch three rows of flat Peyote, odd count. Row 3 will contain 7 (A) beads, row 4 will contain 6 (A) beads and row 5 will contain 7 (A) beads. The rows are numbered in figure 1.

FIGURE 1

Row 6: add 6 beads along the side as if you were stitching another straight row. When you get to the end, instead of turning round, pick up 3 beads and pass through the end bead on the opposite side. Repeat down the other side and step up (18 (A) beads). Figure 2 illustrates the technique although the bead count along the sides is indicative.

FIGURE 2

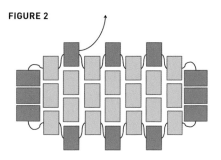

Row 7: you will now continue stitching right around your rectangle, using the hexagon increase pattern for each end. Add 5 (A) along the side, then pick up 2 (A) and pass through the first bead in the group of three at the end. Pick up 2 (A) and pass through the third bead in the end group of three. Pick up 2 (A) and pass through the first up bead on the second side. Add 5 (A) along the second side, then pick up 2 (A) and pass through the first of the three beads at the end. Pick up 2 (A) and pass through the third of the three end beads. Pick up 2 (A) and pass through the last bead and step up ready for the next row (total 22 (A) beads). Figure 3 illustrates the technique although the bead count along the sides is indicative.

FIGURE 3

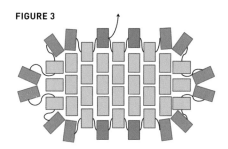

Chocolate Éclair Pendant
I made my eclairs into a pendant and attached it to a
necklace of cellini spiral to give the effect of cream.

Row 8: add one (A) in each space along the sides. Add one (A) in between each of the pairs of beads on the ends (total 22 (A) beads).

Row 9: add one (A) in every space and step up at the end of the row (total 22 (A) beads).

Row 10: you will now be adding a second increase cycle, but change to using the (B) beads. Stitch one bead in every space along the side and add a pair of beads in each of the spaces that contained a pair of beads in row 7. Step up at the end of the row (total 28 (B) beads).

Rows 11 & 12: stitch two more straight rows to complete your increase cycle (total 28 (B) beads).

Rows 13 & 14: Stitch two more straight rows (total 28 (B) beads). This completes one half, so put it to one side.

Repeat rows 1 to 13 to make the second half, but work only in (B) beads as this half will have no chocolate. Add a little bit of stuffing to each half and then join the two halves together. Align the corners and zip up right round the eclair.

Repeat this whole process to make the bottom part of the eclair. Use only (B) beads as there is no chocolate on the

bottom part. When you have completed this part, attach it to the top half. Align the two elements along the back (long) edges and zip them together. Put this to one side while you make the cream filling.

Making the cream:

The cream is made using tubular Peyote stitch, but by picking up the different sized beads in a particular order, you will create a spiral of varying sizes to give the effect of cream. This technique can also be referred to as Cellini spiral.

Rows 1 & 2: leave a tail thread that you can use later for attaching the cream to the éclair. Pick up 4 (C), 2 (D), 2 (E), 2 (D). Pass through all these beads again to form a circle. Pass through the first 4 (C) so that you are exiting from the last (C).

Row 3: using circular Peyote stitch, add 1 (C), 1 (D), 1 (E), 1 (D), 1 (C) and step up (total 2 (C), 2 (D), 1 (E) beads).

Rows 4-30: repeat row three. If you get confused by which bead you will be picking up next, the golden rule is to pick up the same bead as the type from which you have just exited. This gradually forms a spiral.

When you have finished your spiral, press the end flat and stitch it in between the two halves of the éclair. You may wish to anchor the cream along the long edge of the éclair as well. Use your tail thread to stitch the other end together and anchor it in place. Finish off any thread ends and your éclair is complete.

The traditional éclair is made using exactly the same technique, but you only need to make the top part with the chocolate. Add two extra straight rows onto both halves before you zip them up so that this éclair is a little fatter than the individual parts of the cream filled recipe.

Traditional Chocolate Éclair

Mmm...Donuts!

There is some dispute as to the origins of the donut. According to one version, donuts were introduced into North America by Dutch Settlers in the nineteenth century. However, the anthropologist Paul R. Mullins cites an English cookbook of 1803 as being the first to mention this food. The book apparently included an appendix of American recipes, one of which was for the donut. In yet another version of the history, the American, Hansen Gregory, claims that he invented the ring shaped donut in 1847 when he was sailing aboard a lime-trading ship.

Whichever story you like to believe, the donut is now a commonplace food throughout the world, albeit with regional variations.

For those of you partial to a donut or two, you might be interested to know that the first Friday in June is National Donut Day. In 1938 the Salvation Army introduced this memorial to honour the women who had served donuts to soldiers during World War I.

So, if ever you need an excuse for eating a donut, there it is! Failing that, you might like to try making your own beaded versions. My design was inspired by the traditional donut ring, covered in icing and sweet sprinkles and widely found in bakeries, supermarkets and sold by specialists like 'Krispy Kreme' in the US and UK. The design uses circular and tubular Peyote stitch and the shape is created by mixing different sizes of Delicas. I will always associate donuts with May Balls in Cambridge, so I'm dedicating this recipe to some lovely, supportive friends from my university days. For Dan, Eleanor, Jason and Simon – thank you!

INGREDIENTS

2g size 15 Delicas colour DB852 (A)
2g size 11 Delicas colour DB852 (B)
2g size 10 Delicas colour DB852 (C)
1g size 11 Delicas in your chosen icing colour (D)
A handful of size 15 beads in a mix of colours
for the sweet sprinkles
Thread to match your beads

Baking time: 2 hours

RECIPE

Cut a double wingspan of thread. Ordinarily this would be too long to work with comfortably, but I am going to suggest that you leave about one third to half of the thread as a tail thread when you begin working. You will work one half of the donut, then return to the tail thread to work the other half. If you feel uncomfortable working this way, then feel free to cut a comfortable length of thread and join new thread wherever necessary. The whole donut is made using the various DB852 beads. The icing will be made separately at the end.

Rows 1 & 2: Thread twenty four (A). Pass your needle through all twenty four beads again to form a circle. Pass through the first half dozen beads a third time so that the circle is held in place firmly and won't slip as you begin working the next row.

Row 3: begin working in tubular Peyote stitch using the (A) beads. Pick up a bead, pass through the next but one bead in your circle, pick up another bead and pass through the next but one bead in your circle. Repeat until you have added all twelve beads and stitched right around the circle. Step up at the end so that you exit from the first bead you added in row 3 (total 12 (A) beads).

Row 4: continue working in tubular Peyote stitch, adding 1 (A) between each of the beads in row 4. Keep your tension tight and your beads should now be pulling up into a tube, rather than a circle. Remember to step up at the end of the row (total 12 (A) beads).

Rows 5-8: stitch another four rows of tubular Peyote stitch using the (A) beads. Step up at the end of each row (total 12 (A) beads per row).

Row 9: you are now going to start creating the top of your donut, so the tube needs to gradually transform into a circle. Stitch another straight row of tubular Peyote, but this time use the (B) beads. The slightly larger beads will start to make the tube expand. Remember to step up at the end of the row (total 12 (B) beads).

Row 10: stitch another straight row of tubular Peyote using the (B) beads and step up at the end of the row (total 12 (B) beads).

Row 11: the next few rows will be worked in circular Peyote stitch (ie will include increases) so that the beadwork continues to flatten into a circle. Pick up 1 (B) and pass through the next bead from row 10, pick up 2 (B) and pass through the next bead from row 10. Repeat this pattern five more times to take you to the end of the row and step up (total 18 (B) beads). See figure 1.

FIGURE 1

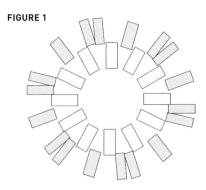

Rows 12 & 13: stitch two straight rows of Peyote stitch using the (B) beads. Step up at the end of each row (total 18 (B) beads per row).

Row 14: this is another increase row. Pick up 1 (B) and pass through the next bead from row 13, pick up 1 (B) and pass through the next bead from row 13, pick up 2 (B) and pass through the next bead from row 13. Repeat this pattern another five times to complete the row and step up at the end. You should notice that each of your increases sits in the space directly over an increase in row 11 (total 24 (B) beads). See figure 2.

FIGURE 2

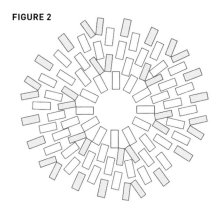

Rows 15 & 16: stitch two more straight rows of Peyote using the (B) beads. Remember to step up at the end of each row (total 24 (B) beads per row).

Rows 17 & 18: it is now time to start creating the outer edge of the donut. Again, this is done by changing bead size. Stitch two straight rows of Peyote stitch using the (C) beads. The change in bead size will continue the circle and graduate into the outer edge. Remember to step up at the end of each row (total 24 (C) beads per row).

Rows 19-24: stitch six rows of straight Peyote stitch using the (C) beads. This will transform the circle back into a tube and form the outer edge of the donut. Figure 3 shows the cross section of the circular shape you have just created. A represents the inner tube, created with the size 15 beads. B represents the top circle created with the size 11 beads. C represents the outer tube, created with the size 10 beads (total 24 (C) beads per row).

FIGURE 3

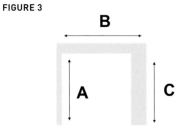

Finish off the thread you have been working with. Now thread your needle onto the long tail thread that is attached to the bottom of the inner tube.

Repeat rows 9 to 16 to create the bottom of the donut, using all (B) beads.

Zip up the outer row of this circle to the bottom of the outer tube of size 10 beads to finish off the donut. Put this to one side while you make the icing.

Icing

To make the icing, use your (D) beads and matching thread.

Rows 1 & 2: pick up 24 (D) and, leaving a short tail thread that can be stitched in later, pass through all 24 beads again. Pass through the first few beads to make sure that the circle sits firmly as you stitch the following rows.

Row 3: pick up 1 (D) and pass through the next but one bead in your circle, pick up 2 (D) and pass through the next but one bead in your circle. Repeat this five more times to complete the row and step up at the end of the row (total 18 (D) beads).

Rows 4 & 5: stitch two straight rows. Step up at the end of each row (total 18 (D) beads per row).

Donut Fridge Magnet
I combined three donuts to create a fridge magnet.

Row 6: this is another increase row. Pick up 1 (D) and pass through the next bead in row 5, pick up 1 (D) and pass through the next bead in row 5, pick up 2 (D) and pass through the next bead in row 5. Repeat this pattern another five times to complete the row. Each pair of beads you have just added should be sitting over the increase you made in row 3. This is exactly the same pattern as you followed to create the top and bottom circles of the donut (total 24 (D) beads).

Rows 7 & 8: stitch two straight rows to complete the circle. Remember to step up at the end of each row (total 24 (D) beads).

Row 9: you are going to effectively stitch an increase row, so add a pair of beads in each space over the previous two increases, but in every third space, instead of adding a bead (or two beads if the space happens to be over an increase), miss the space by passing your needle down through the previous row and exiting out of row 8 (total 20 (D) beads). See figure 4.

FIGURE 4

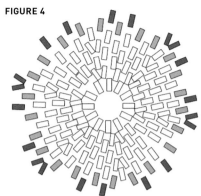

You can either leave the icing plain and stitch it straight onto the top of the donut, or first use your coloured size 15 beads to cover the icing with hundreds and thousands before adding it to the donut. Pass the needle out of a bead in the icing, pick up an (E) bead and pass back through a nearby icing bead. Pass the needle through to exit from another icing bead and add another (E) bead. Continue until you have added as much decoration as you want.

I have made my donuts into pendants, necklaces, fridge magnets, key rings and ornaments – the possibilities are endless, so use your imagination and enjoy!

Donut Pendant
A single donut makes a great pendant.

Donut Necklace
I used split rings to link a series of donuts into a necklace and put it on a spiral stitch chain.

CHAPTER 6

MIXING BEAD TYPES

The two projects in this section both mix different varieties of beads. In each case, the style of bead is intended to represent a component of the cake, eg chocolate chips, but the beading challenge lies in seamlessly integrating these different varieties.

The blackforest gateau uses circular and tubular Peyote and also freeform bead embroidery. The peanut beads, bugles and round beads are all added to a Delica base to represent the distinctive decoration on the cake. **The chocolate chip cookies** are made using Brick stitch and integrate cubes with Delica beads to mimic the chocolate chips in the cookie dough.

Blackforest Gateau   page 66

page 70

Chocolate Chip Cookies

Blackforest Gateau

Blackforest Gateau, or Scharzwalderkirschtorte, to give it its German name, is the best-selling cake in Germany and is also popular worldwide in different variations. The first recipe for this cake was published in 1934, but it certainly dates back further than that. It is rumoured that the name comes from the Kirsch drink that gives the authentic gateau its distinctive flavour.

I developed this recipe immediately after I had developed my recipes for miniature celebration cakes. I was fascinated with the idea of using different bead varieties for decorating my cakes and at around that time, Peanut Beads first appeared in the UK. For some reason, they reminded me of the chocolate shavings that are often used to decorate the top of this gateau. I then realised that bugle beads would make perfect chocolate sprinkles and round red beads looked exactly like cherries. I made a basic cake and then used all these different beads to create the decoration, adding some cream swirls as a finishing touch. This happens to be one of my brother's favourite cakes, so this recipe is for him, with lots of love!

INGREDIENTS

Per Cake:
15g size 11 Delicas in DB201 for the cake base (A)
6g size 11 Delicas in DB041 for the cake board (B)
10g 2x4mm Peanut Beads in Matte Metallic Dark Raspberry
10g 3mm Bugles in Bronze
2g size 8 beads in Ceylon White (C)
2g size 11 beads in Ceylon White (D)
2g size 15 beads in Ceylon White (E)
17 6mm round beads in Red
Thread to match or tone with your beads

Baking time: 10 hours

RECIPE

This cake is made with a flat Peyote stitch hexagon for the top, continuing into tubular Peyote stitch to make the sides. The cake board is then added and, finally, the beads that will give the effect of chocolate decoration and the cream and cherries to finish.

Make a flat Peyote stitch hexagon, continuing to stitch until you have 60 beads in a row and have completed the final increase cycle. Make sure that you are familiar with the hexagon increase pattern before you begin this project. The bead count in each row will be as follows:

Row 1: 3 (A) beads

Row 2: 6 (A) beads – this is an increase row

Row 3: 6 (A) beads

Row 4: 12 (A) beads – this is an increase row

Rows 5 & 6: 12 (A) beads

Row 7: 18 (A) beads – this is an increase row

Rows 8 & 9: 18 (A) beads

Row 10: 24 (A) beads - this is an increase row

Rows 11 & 12: 24 (A) beads

Row 13: 30 (A) beads – this is an increase row

Rows 14 & 15: 30 (A) beads

Row 16: 36 (A) beads – this is an increase row

Rows 17 & 18: 36 (A) beads

Row 19: 42 (A) beads – this is an increase row

Rows 20 & 21: 42 (A) beads

Row 22: 48 (A) beads – this is an increase row

Rows 23 & 24: 48 (A) beads

Row 25: 54 (A) beads – this is an increase row

Rows 26 & 27: 54 (A) beads

Row 28: 60 (A) beads – this is an increase row

Rows 29 & 30: 60 (A) beads – this completes your final cycle

Rows 31-52: 60 (A) beads

Change to the (B) beads to make the cake board. The bead count is as follows:

Row 53: 66 (D) beads – this is an increase row

Row 54 & 55: 66 (D) beads

Row 56: 72 (D) beads – this is an increase row

Rows 57 & 58: 72 (D) beads

Row 59: 78 (D) beads – this is an increase row

Row 60: 78 (D) beads

Add the card and felt backing, following the instructions on page 29.

Rows 61-65: 78 (D) beads to take the beads down over the edges of the cake board and give it a good finish.

The Decoration

For the decoration, first make the twelve swirls of cream with cherries on top. The cream is made using tubular Peyote stitch as follows – the combination of different sized beads creates a small spiral that gives the effect of whipped cream.

Rows 1 & 2: pick up 6 (E), 2 (D), 2 (C), 6 (E), 2 (D), 2 (C). Pass through all the beads again to form them into a circle and exit from the second (C) bead.

Row 3: stitch a row of Peyote stitch (ie pick up a bead, pass through the next but one bead in row 1, etc, and step up at the end of the row) picking the beads up in the following order – 1 (C), 3 (E), 1 (D), 1 (C), 3 (E), 1 (D). After the 'step up' you should have exited from the first size 8 (C bead) in row 3.

Rows 4-6: repeat row 3, keeping the order of beads exactly the same (if you find yourself getting confused, pick up a bead that is the same as the bead you just exited).

Row 7: stitch another row the same, but decrease 1 in the middle of each group of size 15s, so you will have just added a (C), exiting from an (E), pick up 1 (E), pass through the next two (E) beads, pick up 1 (E) and pass through the next (D) bead (total 2 (C), 2 (D), 4 (E) beads).

Row 8: this is another straight row, so add 1 (C), 2 (E), 1 (D), 1 (C), 2 (E), 1 (D) and step up to exit from the first size 8.

Add a cherry: pick up a 6mm round red bead and pass through the size 8 bead on the opposite side of your tube of cream.

Pass your needle and thread back through the cream to exit from somewhere in the first row. Position the cream with cherry on the top of the cake so that it sits at the iced edge and stitch it securely onto the cake

Repeat this whole process to make the remaining swirls of cream with a cherry and secure them onto the gateau so that they sit evenly around the outer edge of the cake.

Add a group of five cherries to the centre of the cake, then complete the rest of the decoration.

You will now add chocolate sprinkles to the outer iced edge of the cake and chocolate shavings to the top of the cake. The technique is the same for both: exit from a bead in the white icing, pick up a single chocolate bead and pass through a single bead in the icing, near the bead from which you exited, but so that the chocolate bead sits flat on the icing. Keep repeating until the cake surface is evenly covered. If you still have unfinished lengths of thread anywhere on the cake, you can use these to stitch the chocolate beads, then finish the thread securely.

Use the peanut beads for the chocolate shavings on the top of the cake and the bugle beads for the chocolate sprinkles on the side of the cake.

I used white thread so that it would blend with the icing at the edges of the chocolate beads. Make sure you have an even covering of chocolate, but don't worry if the white icing still peeps through – it would do on a real cake.

Once you have covered all your edges and the top, your cake is finished.

The Gateau Keyring

I designed a slice of gateau for the Beadworker's Guild. This appeared in their journal in April 2011. I have since made up more of these to use as fridge magnets, key rings and handbag charms. The recipe uses the same technique as the slice of Victoria Sponge, but I have changed my bead colours to illustrate where you would see the cake in a slice and where the icing would be visible. The real gateau also has a layer (or multiple) layers of cream between the sponge, so that is reflected in my design.

The Gateau Keyring

Chocolate Chip Cookies

Chocolate chip cookies were accidentally invented by Ruth Graves Wakefield in the 1930s. Working at the Toll House Inn in Massachusetts, Ruth was part way through baking a batch of chocolate cookies when she realised that she had run out of regular baking chocolate. She had a batch of broken pieces of chocolate made by Nestle, so she added these to her mixture, expecting that they would simply melt and mix into the batter as the cookies baked. Imagine her surprise when she removed the cookies from the oven and discovered that she had created an entirely new recipe. Ruth reputedly sold her recipe to Nestle in exchange for a life-time supply of chocolate chips!

I have to thank Johannes for the idea behind this design. He suggested making giant chocolate chip cookies and I thought they would be immediately recognisable and also translate really well into unusual jewellery and ornaments. However, it took me a while to work out this design. I knew from the beginning that I wanted to use 4mm cube beads for the chocolate chips, but this left the problem of how to integrate these seamlessly with the smaller seed beads. I initially began experimenting with circular herringbone, but that did not prove successful, so I ended up turning to brick stitch for the answer. As you will see, I have managed to find a way of combining size 10 Delicas with 4mm cube beads. If you want to make earrings or smaller cookies, then keep to the same pattern, but scale down the bead size and work with 1.8mm cube beads and size 15 Delicas. This recipe is quite free-form, so I would recommend familiarising yourself with the instructions before you start making it. I am dedicating the recipe to Johannes with thanks for showing me so much kindness and support.

INGREDIENTS

Per Cookie:
Approximately 30 4mm cubes in chocolate brown
5g size 10 delicas DB852
Thread to match or tone with your beads
A small amount of gold or cream coloured material
to stuff the cookie

Baking time: 90 minutes

RECIPE

Each cookie is made using circular brick stitch. You will need to make two halves and then stitch them together.

Begin by picking up a cube bead. Leaving a short tail that you can stitch in at the end, knot your thread so that it sits round the cube bead. Pass your needle through the bead again, so that this new thread sits round the opposite side of your bead. Knot the thread to hold this second side in place (see figure 1). Make sure that the thread is pulled tight against the bead – this is going to be the base upon which you stitch your first row of brick stitch.

FIGURE 1

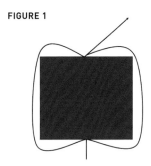

In straight brick stitch, the beads sit in a brick pattern, as the name suggests, so for every two beads in a row, there will be 3 beads sitting on top in the next row, each ending halfway along the bead beneath it (see figure 2). For circular or curved brick stitch, the technique and the idea is the same, but because of the curve, the number of beads in each additional row will increase. This means that at various points around the curve, you will need to increase a bead. Compare the beads in the curved

FIGURE 2

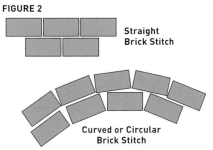

Straight
Brick Stitch

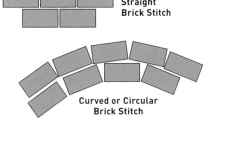

Curved or Circular
Brick Stitch

example in figure 2: whereas in the straight sample, the second row has one extra bead to the first row, in the curved sample, you need more beads to create the second row. It is difficult to specify exactly where to increase – if you want to create an even circle, you will need to spread your increase beads evenly round the circle. Increasing all in one place gives a bulge. You can generally see where you need to increase – the distance to the next thread under which you would normally pass becomes too far to reach comfortably – this is a sign to increase. If you increase too often you will find that your circle starts to pleat instead of laying flat. If you increase too little, the circle starts to pull inwards. For the cookies, it is best to allow the circle to pull inwards very slightly.

For the first row, you will use the thread you have just added around the cube bead to pass your needle under in order to create a row of brick stitch. Pick up 2 Delicas, pass your needle under the thread and back up through the second of your two beads. Pick up one Delica, pass your needle under the thread and back up through your bead (figure 3).

FIGURE 3

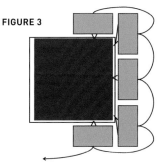

Continue all the way around the cube bead. The row will contain 8 or 9 beads. As you reach the hole in the cube bead, you will find that there is no thread across it. If you can stretch across to the other side of the hole, then do this. If this feels like too big a stretch, then add another bead using the thread on the side of the hole on which you are working, before stretching across the hole. Adjust your beads as you work so that they sit evenly around the cube bead. When you reach the end of the row, after exiting from your last bead, pass down through the next Delica so that the first and last beads are joined up. Continue to pass down through the cube bead and exit from a Delica on the opposite side of the cube. This helps to hold your first row in place and is easier than trying to exit from an adjacent Delica on the first side. You are now ready to begin the second row.

Stitch a second row in exactly the same way as you did the first row (remember to start by picking up 2 beads). Increase as you go around this row. Try and keep the increases spread evenly around the row – you should end up with around 13 beads in this row (12 or 14 should be fine).

In row 3 you will start adding chocolate chips (cube beads). The cube beads are a different size to the Delicas, so there is a special technique for weaving them seamlessly into your brick stitch.

To add a chocolate chip: as you exit from the Delica, pick up one Delica and one cube bead. Pass your needle under the next thread and back up through the cube bead. Pick up two Delicas. Pass your needle under the thread and back up through the bottom Delica only. You should now have a stack of two Delicas on either side of the cube bead (see figure 4) – you may need to ease the Delicas into position. Continue round the row by picking up one Delica at a time as usual.

FIGURE 4

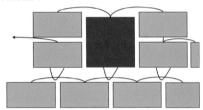

When you stitch the next row, you will find that you already have part of it in place – created by the additional Delicas and cube bead. Brick stitch as normal up to the point at which you meet the existing Delica. Pass down through that Delica and the one beneath it and take your thread along to pass back up through the two Delicas on the other side of the cube, exiting from the top Delica so you are ready to continue along your row. As you do this, make sure that you pull your thread really tight so that it sits invisibly between the beads at the base of the cube (see figure 5).

FIGURE 5

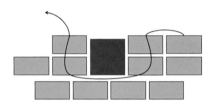

To finish the first half of the cookie, stitch seven rows. Keep increasing in each row and add chocolate chips as you go. I try and keep the chocolate chips randomly spaced, allowing some to touch each other or sit very close by just as they would if you were baking real cookies. Remember that each chocolate chip spans two rows, so you cannot add any chips in row 7. As a tip, try not to add a chocolate chip where the brick stitch needs to increase; just make your increase and then add the chocolate chip on your next stitch.

Once you have finished the first half, secure the end of your thread, but don't cut it off – you may want to use it for joining the two halves.

Put this completed half to one side and make another half in exactly the same way.

Joining the two halves Put your two cookie halves together – if they have a slight curve, then make sure that both halves are curving outwards to give the cookie some shape. If you have chocolate chips near the edge of your cookie halves, than think about the placement so that these edge chips are positioned away from each other and not all in the same place. Using the thread from one or other of your cookie halves, pick up two Delicas and, holding the two halves together, pass down through a Delica in the final row of the other half. Pass back up through the next Delica in this half. Pick up two more Delicas and pass down through the Delica next to the one from which you started in your first half. Pass back up through the next Delica in your first half, pick up two Delicas and repeat the process moving back to your second half. Continue this process all the way around the cookies, so that you zip up the two halves. When you have stitched just over half way around the cookie, stuff it with a little material to give it some body. Continue stitching to the end and then finish off any threads.

If you want, you can pick up a cube bead instead of the two delicas so that you have a chocolate chip sitting at the edge of your cookie. As you are stitching, you may find that you reach a chocolate chip in the final row of one or other half. In this case you will not be able to stitch down and back up before moving across to the other half. Instead, simply pass your needle under the thread at the top of the chocolate chip (as if you were doing Brick Stitch) and then pick up two Delicas and pass back to the other half as usual.

Cookies Jewellery Set
I stitched two cookies together to form a pendant. I made the earrings on a smaller scale, so used 1.8mm cube beads and size 15 Delicas.

White and Dark Chocolate
Use different coloured beads to make different varieties of cookie.

Cookies and Cream
Fridge Magnet.

TIP: If you run out of thread part way through joining the two halves, either switch to using the left over thread from your other half or simply join a new thread.

Try playing with colour to make different varieties of cookie. To make double chocolate chip cookies, I used Delica bead colour 312 for the dough and the same brown cubes.

If you want to make white chocolate chip cookies, then use cube beads in Cream Ceylon.

If you decide to make a fridge magnet, you will need to incorporate the magnet into the cookie as you work.

Make one half of the cookie as normal, but stitch 10 rows of brick stitch instead of 7.

Cover your fridge magnet with the material. (See the instructions on page 26).

Begin the second half of your cookie by stitching the base row of brick stitch to the material round the fridge magnet. The principle is the same, but you will need to pass through a tiny bit of material instead of passing under a thread. Stitch a further 7 rows as normal. You should find that your two halves are now the same size – the fridge magnet, because of its size, equates to the first three rows of brick stitch. Check that the two halves match and then join them as usual.

Incorporate the fridge magnet into one half of your bottom cookie.

To make a cookies and cream fridge magnet, you will need to make the fridge magnet as outlined above. Then make a second cookie, without a magnet, but stitch ten rows and not seven. Next, make a strip of cream long enough to reach half way around a cookie. Use the Cellini spiral technique I used for making cream in the Chocolate Eclairs recipe.

Finally, assemble this by stitching the cream on top of the cookie with the magnet (make sure that the magnet is underneath), so that it follows the curve of the cookie and sits just slightly in from the edge. Place the second cookie on top and stitch it in place so that it is attached to the bottom cookie at the top and the top of the strip of cream around the front. Stitch as neatly as possible so that your stitches cannot be seen. Your cookies and cream magnet is complete.

CHAPTER 7
MIXING BEAD STITCHES

This section focuses on projects that use a combination of two stitches and integrates those different stitches within a single piece of beadwork.

The jam tarts start in one drop Peyote stitch and move seamlessly to two drop Peyote. **The Bakewell tarts** combine circular Peyote and even count straight Peyote. These two projects are a slight cheat in that they are in fact combining different versions of the same stitch. **The cupcakes** use a Brick stitch base and then converts to tubular Peyote for the top and bottom.

Jam Tarts page 76

Bakewell Medley page 80

Cupcakes page 84

Jam Tarts

Jam tarts have evolved from the traditional English pie which can be traced back to 1303 when the first known use of the word 'pie' was recorded. Tarts were open pies that became popular in Medieval times. They could be savoury, but were often sweet, frequently containing egg custard and fruits of various kinds. These kinds of open pastries, filled with egg custard and fruit are still commonplace in European cake shops. The jam tart, a small pastry case filled with jam – usually strawberry, but it can also be blackcurrant or apricot jam - seems to be peculiarly English. One of its most well-known associations has to come from Lewis Carroll's 'Alice in Wonderland' in which the Queen of Hearts tries the Knave of Hearts for the crime of stealing a plate of Jam Tarts.

I have long struggled with trying to find a technique that can create a really round circle, but not result in beadwork that crinkles or refuses to lie flat. The hexagonal Peyote stitch that I have used for other recipes comes close, but it can be hard to prevent the increase pattern from turning into corners, so the cakes are never truly round. Mixing bead sizes, as I have done for my donuts pattern, helps to overcome this problem, but in this instance, I thought I would try a different technique entirely. The problem seemed to come from the way in which a Peyote increase is formed, so I thought I would try using a partial increase, so adding two beads in a space, but not then adding a bead between them in the following row. Instead, I found myself gradually moving from a pattern of one-drop Peyote to two-drop Peyote. It seemed to result in a more rounded circle, but I think it has limitations in that it works best on a small size. So, have a go – in essence the idea is simple, but take care not to get confused over which beads to pass through when you are in the process of transitioning between the two stitches. I am dedicating this pattern to Lauren, with huge thanks for her support and inspiration on my journey back to good health.

INGREDIENTS

Per jam tart:
2g size 11 Delicas in DB852 (A)
1g size 11 Delicas in DB295 (B)
Thread to match or tone with your beads – you may
want to use different threads for the jam and the pastry

Baking time: 45 minutes

RECIPE

Begin by making the pastry base. Working with a comfortable thread length and your (A) beads, you will be using circular Peyote stitch.

Row 1: pick up 3 (A) and tie the ends of your thread together to form the beads into a circle. Leave a tail thread that is long enough for you to stitch in at the end.

Row 2: add 2 (A) between each of your beads in row 1 and remember to step up at the end of the row (total 6 (A) beads).

Row 3: add 1 (A) between each of the beads in row 2 and step up at the end of the row (total 6 (A) beads).

Row 4: add 2 beads in each space and step up at the end of the row (total 12 (A) beads).

Rows 5 & 6: add 1 bead between each of the beads in the previous row and remember to step up at the end of each row (total 12 (A) beads).

Row 7: add 1 bead in the first space, add 2 beads in the next space. Repeat this pattern all around the row and step up at the end of the row (total 18 (A) beads).

Row 8: this is the point at which you start to convert to two-drop Peyote stitch, so take care to ensure you know where you are passing through a single bead from the previous row and where you are passing through a pair of beads – you will not be adding beads in between the pairs you added in row 7. Add 2 (A) in the first space and pass through a pair of beads from row 7. Add 1 (A) in the second space and pass through a single bead from row 7. Repeat this pattern round the rest of the row. When you step up at the end of the row, make sure you step up through both beads in the first pair that you added (total 18 (A) beads).

FIGURE 1

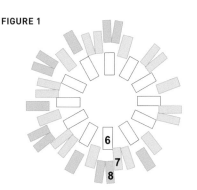

Figure 1 shows the start of the transition row from one-drop to two-drop Peyote stitch. The numbers on the diagram correspond to the row numbers. Note how you pass through a pair of beads from row 7 each time, rather than employing the conventional Peyote increase of adding a bead between the pairs.

Row 9: add 2 (A) in the first space and pass through a single bead from row 8. Add 1 (A) in the second space and pass through a pair of beads from row 8. Repeat all the way around this row and step up through the original pair of beads at the end of the row (total 18 (A) beads).

Row 10: add 2 (A) in every space, but in the first space you will pass through a single bead, in the second space you will pass through a pair of beads. Maintain this sequence for the entire row and step up through a pair of beads at the end of the row (total 24 (A) beads).

Rows 11-13: for these three rows you will be working in full two-drop Peyote stitch, so add 2 (A) in each space and pass through a pair of beads from the previous row each time. Step up through a pair of beads at the end of the row (total 24 (A) beads).

Put the pastry base to one side, but do not finish off your working thread – you will come back to use it again when you have added the jam to the base.

A plate of Jam Tarts

Jam Filling

Make the jam filling using the (B) beads and a comfortable length of thread to match or tone with the beads. Repeat rows 1 to 11 exactly as you made the base. By omitting rows 12 and 13 you will end up with a flat circle instead of a circle with short sides.

Take your pastry base and hold the jam in the top of it, matching the beads so that the final row of pastry beads interlocks with the final row of jam beads. Zip the two pieces together and finish off the thread you were using to make the jam filling.

Thread your needle back onto the thread you were using for the pastry base and, once again use the (A) beads to stitch two more rows as follows.

Row 14: add 3 (A) in each space in the previous row of pastry and step up at the end of the row, passing through all three of the beads you added at the start of the row (total 36 (A) beads).

Row 15: add 2 (A) in each space, passing through all three beads from row 14 on each stitch (total 24 (A) beads). These two rows will give your pastry base the uneven edge that one would expect to find on a jam tart. Finish off your thread and the tart is complete and ready to use.

Turn one into a key ring, or use several together to make a necklace, pendant or bracelet. You might also like to try using different bead sizes to make smaller or larger versions. You can use orange transparent beads to create an apricot tart, or deep purple transparent beads for the blackcurrant variety.

Apricot Tart
Use transparent orange beads to make an apricot tart. I turned this one into a key ring.

Jam Tart Necklace

I used a series of three jam tarts to make a focal centre for a necklace.
I strung this onto heart-shaped beads to follow
the 'Alice in Wonderland' theme.

Bakewell Medley

Serena suggested that the lattice work on top of a Bakewell Tart would make an interesting beaded treat, so I decided to give it a go and investigate further. I discovered that the Bakewell Tart actually has a rather interesting history. Bakewell Pudding was first made by accident at the Whitehorse Inn in Bakewell in 1820. The owner of the Inn one day went out, leaving instructions for the cook to make a jam tart. However, instead of stirring an egg and almond paste into the pastry mixture, the cook mistakenly spread it on top of the jam before cooking the tart. When the tart was cooked, this mixture set like egg custard. This new dish was served up to customers and it became a very popular dish at the Inn. Hence this English dessert was born.

Bakewell Tart is a pastry shell, spread with jam and covered with frangipane (a sponge-like filling enriched with ground almonds). Lattice work or nuts can be added to the top. There is also a Cherry Bakewell variation where the frangipane is covered with icing and decorated with half a glace cherry. The true Bakewell tart is native to the town of Bakewell in Derbyshire.

Having discovered all these variations, I decided to combine them into a Bakewell Medley. The open tart with no covering is made using the recipe I developed for my Jam Tarts. Just use DB709 Delica beads to make the filling instead of the red beads. The mini Cherry Bakewells are made in two halves using circular Peyote stitch, incorporating the cherry into the icing as you stitch. The Bakewell Tart with its lattice work is, once again, a simple circular Peyote base, but the lattice work is added by stitching strips of even count Peyote across the top of the tart. So, thank you to Serena for a great idea. Thank you for many years of wonderful friendship and for always being there.

INGREDIENTS

Per Cherry Bakewell:
1g size 11 Delicas in DB852 for the base (A)
1g size 11 Delicas in DB231 for the icing (B)
1 x 4mm round bead in red
Thread to match or tone with your beads

Baking time: 30 minutes

Per Bakewell Tart:
3g size 11 Delicas in DB852 for the pastry (A)
1g size 11 Delicas in DB709 for the filling (C)
Thread to match or tone with your beads

Baking time: 90 minutes

RECIPE

Cherry Bakewell

This cake is made in two halves – the pastry filling and the icing – which are then stitched together. Both halves are made using circular Peyote stitch and employing the hexagon increase pattern.

Begin by making the pastry base.

Row 1: working with a comfortable length of thread and your (A) beads, pick up 3 beads. Leaving a tail thread that you can stitch in at the end, tie the two ends of your thread together so that your beads form a circle.

Row 2: add 2 beads between each of the beads in your initial circle and step up at the end of the row (total 6 (A) beads).

Row 3: add 1 bead between each of the beads in the previous row and step up at the end of the row (total 6 (A) beads).

Row 4: add 2 beads in each space and step up at the end of the row (total 12 (A) beads).

Rows 5 & 6: add 1 bead between each of the beads in the previous row and step up at the end of the row (total 12 (A) beads).

Row 7: this is an increase row. Add 1 bead in the first space and 2 beads in the second space. Repeat this pattern round the rest of the row and step up at the end (total 18 (A) beads).

Rows 8-12: stitch five straight rows, ie adding one bead in each space and stepping up at the end of each row (total 18 (A) beads). Finish off your thread and put the pastry base to one side.

Icing

Thread your 4mm round bead and then pick up 6 (B) beads. Pass your needle through the round bead so that the (B) beads sit along one side of it.

Pick up another 6 (B) and pass your needle through the round bead again. The (B) beads should now encircle your round bead (see figure 1).

FIGURE 1

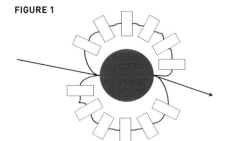

Pass your needle through all twelve of the (B) beads a couple of times so that the circle of small beads sits tightly around the round bead. Now start working in circular Peyote stitch using the 12 (B) beads as your foundation row.

Row 1: pick up 2 (B), skip a bead in the foundation row and pass through the next bead. Repeat all the way around the row and step up at the end to exit from the first bead in your first pair of beads (total 12 beads). The start of this row is illustrated in figure 2.

FIGURE 2

Rows 2 & 3: stitch 2 straight rows of Peyote, so add 1 (B) between each bead in your previous row (total 12 (B) beads).

Row 4: stitch an increase row. Add 1 (B) in the first space and 2 (B) in the next space and so on round the entire row (total 18 (B) beads).

Row 5: stitch a straight row using the (B) beads (total 18 (B) beads).

Now take the pastry base and hold your icing in place so that the last row of beads on the icing interlocks with the top row of beads on the base. Do not worry about trying to match up corners – the cake wants to be rounded, so if the corners formed by the increases in the icing do not match the corners formed by the increases in the base, this effect is likely to be more easily achieved. Zip up the two rows. Finish off any threads and your Cherry Bakewell is complete. The Cherry Bakewell should hold its shape, but if you want to make it more solid, stuff a small piece of tissue into the pastry base before you join the icing to the base.

Bakewell Tart

The tart is also made in two halves: the bottom pastry case and then the top filling and lattice work. The two halves are then joined together to finish off.

Begin by making the base. Use the (A) beads and you will be stitching a circular Peyote stitch with the hexagon increase pattern.

Rows 1-9: follow rows 1 to 9 for the Cherry Bakewell base pattern.

Row 10: stitch another increase row. Add 2 (A) in the first space, 1 (A) in the second space and 1 (A) in the third space and repeat this pattern right around the row, stepping up at the end (total 24 (A) beads).

Rows 11-14: stitch 4 straight rows of Peyote, adding 1 (A) in each space and stepping up at the end of each row (total 24 (A) beads per row). This completes your base, so put this to one side.

The top of the tart is made in exactly the same way as the base, but the final two rows of straight Peyote are replaced with the lattice work.

Rows 1-10: use the (C) beads and follow the pattern for the pastry base.

Rows 11 & 12: keep following the pattern for the pastry base, but use the (A) beads for these two rows.

You are now going to work another row in circular Peyote to create a foundation for the lattice work. The lattice itself is formed from a series of strips of Peyote, starting one side of the cake and joining to a base bead in the opposite side. There are six strips in total. The first three you work will lay flat across the tart and the last three will weave over and under the first three.

Row 13: this row creates the foundation for the lattice work. Add 1(A) in the first space, then miss out the next space. The thread path is illustrated in figure 3. Continue all the way around the row (total 12 (A) beads).

FIGURE 3

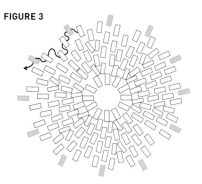

When you have added the last bead in row 13, pass down through the bead immediately to its left and exit from this bead. This is illustrated by the red thread path in figure 4.

FIGURE 4

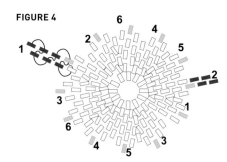

Pick up 1(A) and pass through the foundation bead. Pick up 1(A) and pass through the bead you just added. Pick up 1(A) and pass through the bead you just added. Maintain this zigzag pattern (see the black thread path in figure 4) until you have added 24 beads and formed a strip of straight Peyote stitch.

Attach the strip to its opposite foundation bead, making sure that you attach the final bead to the left hand side of the foundation bead. This first strip is marked '1' in figure 4 and the point to which it will be joined is also labelled with a '1'. To attach the strip, you will pass from right to left through the foundation bead.

Bakewell Magnet
I combined one of each variety of Bakewell to make a fridge magnet.

Then follow the thread path illustrated in figure 5 (or create your own thread path, but make sure that it remains true to the natural Peyote path) so that you exit from the bead to the left of the foundation bead next to your strip (marked 2 in the diagrams).

FIGURE 5

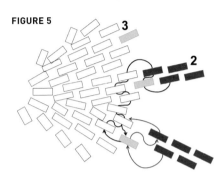

Continue to stitch another strip exactly as you did the first, but this time, add just 22 beads. This is strip 2 and is marked in figure 4. Once again join this strip to a foundation bead on the other side of the tart, but note that this bead sits to the right of strip 1. This means that you are sitting across a slightly narrower part of the tart, hence the need for fewer beads in this strip. Work your way through to start strip 3, following a similar thread path, but this strip starts from the foundation bead immediately on the left of the first strip, so your thread path will be a little longer.

Strip 3 will also be 22 beads long and will join across the tart so that it sits beside strip 1.

Work your way round the edge of the tart to the central foundation bead of the three that are left. Work a strip of 24 beads, but this time weave your strip over the top of strip 2, under strip 1 and over the top of strip 3 before joining it to the opposite central foundation bead.

Work your way through to the next foundation bead to stitch strip 5. This is a side strip, so contains 22 beads. Weave this strip under strip 3, over the top of strip 1 and under strip 2 before joining it to its foundation bead. (See figure 6).

FIGURE 6

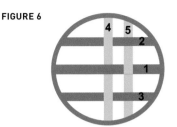

Work the final strip as a length of 22 beads and weave it under strip 2, over the top of strip 1 and under strip 3 before joining it into place.

Finally, add the top to the base. Place the base so that its top row beads interlock with the beads in row 11 of the top (this is the first row of (A) beads). Zip the two edges together to join the two halves and finish off any threads to complete your tart.

Bakewell Tart Necklace & Bracelet
I made a necklace and bracelet set by using sealed jump rings to join the different tarts into a sequence.

Cupcakes

The origin of the cupcake is unknown, but recipes for these little treats have been printed since at least as far back as the late eighteenth Century. The idea behind them seems to have been to create individual portions of cake. In the nineteenth Century they became commonly known as 'Cupcakes' after the pottery cups or ramekins in which they were baked. They were also known in England as 'Fairy Cakes'. Traditionally, these are slightly smaller than cupcakes and are not topped with elaborate icing. My grandmother used to bake these with just a couple of small wedges of sponge on top, held on with a small blob of icing. Today, cupcakes have turned into a huge industry with ever more elaborate finishes.

The inspiration for this design came from a tiny café in Covent Garden, London. I've walked past this many times on my way between bead shops in the area. The window is full of little cupcakes with the most colourful icing and decoration. The décor in the café itself is similarly colourful and fun and it looks so inviting! The design is a combination of Brick stitch and Peyote stitch. It took me a long time and several experiments to reach a design that I felt worked to achieve the slightly slanted sides of the cake, the grooves that always result from the baking cases and just the right spiral of coloured icing on top. Having decided early on that only Brick Stitch would give me the shape I wanted for the cake, whilst I would need to use Peyote stitch to create the spiral of icing, I then had to find a way of seamlessly combining the two stitches. I think this method works pretty well, so I hope you will enjoy creating these little temptations. I'm dedicating the recipe to Heather, a friend who has recovered from ME and been very supportive of me over the past few years.

INGREDIENTS

2g size 10 Delicas in colour DB0852 (A)
1g size 8 seed beads in icing colour (B)
1g size 11 seed beads in icing colour (C)
Thread

Baking Time: 2 hours
I like to use two different shades of the same colour
for the icing, so this could be a dark pink and a slightly
lighter pink, or it could be a silver lined bead and
a matte bead in the same shade. You can also use
exactly the same colour of bead, just in different sizes.

RECIPE

Work with a wingspan of thread and leave a 6" (15cm) tail.

Row 1: Thread a row of ladder stitch, 24 beads long, using the (A) beads. At the end of the row, join the two ends to form a circle. Be very careful that you have not twisted the beads when you create the join.

Row 2: Make sure that your tail thread is exiting from the bottom of your circle of beads and your working thread is exiting from the top. If this is not the case, simply thread your working thread through to the top of the circle, leaving the tail thread at the bottom. Stitch a row of Brick stitch on top of your ladder stitch base. You will need to increase three beads in this row (total 27 beads), so stich as follows:

Pick up two beads to start your brick stitch. Add another six beads of normal brick stitch.

As you add the ninth bead, make this an increase, so pass your thread under the same spot as you used to attach the previous bead. (If you are unsure, refer back to the brick stitch instructions in chapter 2).

Add another eight beads of straight brick stitch, but be careful to make sure that you add the first of these beads in the space next to your increase – it can be easy to miss this space if your increase bead is sitting slightly on top of it.

The ninth bead will be another increase bead – again, be careful to ensure that you are passing your needle under the correct thread when you add both this bead and also the next straight bead.

Stitch a final eight straight beads and then add the last increase bead in the final space at the end of your row. Ease all your beads into place so that the row sits straight and you can just begin to see the slant of the rows for the cake.

FIGURE 1

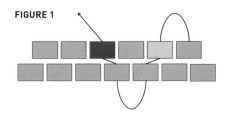

Pass your thread down through the first bead in this row (shown in green in figure 1), down through the bead diagonally to the left in the row beneath, then back up through the next bead to the left in the bottom row and diagonally to the left to exit from the top bead (shown in red in figure 1).

You are doing this so that you start the next row slightly further along than the start of your second row. As you will be adding more increases, this ensures that the increase beads are spread round the sides and not one on top of the other. If they were stitched directly above one another, then the cake would start to form an uneven slope.

Row 3: Add another row with three increase beads (total 30 (A) beads), so follow the same process as for row two, but this time stitch nine straight beads and increase on the tenth bead.

Row 4: This row also increases in the same way (total 33 (A) beads). Again, repeat the increase pattern, but stitch ten straight beads and increase on the eleventh.

Row 5: is the final increase row (total 36 (A) beads). This time, stitch eleven straight beads and increase on the twelfth bead.

Row 6: is a row of straight brick stitch (total 36 (A) beads).

To allow you to change from Brick Stitch to Peyote stitch, you will need to add a picot edge around the top of your cake. Pick up one (A) pass down through the next bead in row six and up through the next bead. Repeat all the way around the cupcake (see figure 2). You should have added 18 (A) beads. Finish off your thread.

FIGURE 2

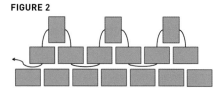

The base of the cupcake is also going to be made using Peyote stitch as this creates a flatter, more even circle than I have been able to achieve with Brick stitch. Therefore you will need a Picot edge on the bottom to allow you to attach the base you are about to make to the sides. Thread your needle onto the tail thread and repeat the method you used in step seven, to add twelve beads round the base of the cake (see figure 2). Finish your thread and put the cake to one side.

The base is made using circular Peyote stitch. Again, work with a wingspan of thread, but this time leave a tail thread just long enough for you to stitch in securely at the end.

Row 1: Pick up 3 (A) beads and pass through them again to create a circle. Make sure your tension is tight so that the circle does not pull apart as you work the subsequent rows – knot the ends of your thread to secure this if you prefer.

Row 2: Add 2 (A) between each bead in your first circle (6 (A) beads). Step up at the end ready to start the next row.

Row 3: Add 1 (A) between each bead in the previous row (6 (A) beads). Remember to step up at the end of the row.

Row 4: Add 2 (A) in each space (12 (A) beads). Step up.

Row 5: Add 1 (A) in between each bead in your previous row (12 (A) beads) and step up.

Take your cake and place this circular base on the bottom. Zip up the beads in your last row of the base to the twelve beads in the picot edge. Maintain a good tension so that the base is pulled tightly into the sides. This will also help to give some stability to your brick stitch sides.

Pass your needle up through the side of the cake and exit from one of the picot edge beads at the top of the cake. You will now add the icing.

Row 1: Add 1 (B) bead between each bead in the picot edge (18 (B) beads). Step up at the end to exit from your first (B) bead. You will find that this begins to pull the cake inwards slightly – this is absolutely correct.

Row 2: Add one bead in each space in row 1, in the following order: 1(B), 1(C), 1(C). Repeat this six times and step up at the end of the row (total 6(B) and 12(C) beads).

Rows 3-6: Repeat row 2. You will notice that the beads are beginning to spiral round. This is the effect you are aiming to achieve, so do not attempt to alter the order in which you add beads. The golden rule to maintain for the whole icing is 'always pick up a bead that is the same as the bead you have just exited'. If you lose your place in the stitching or are getting confused as to the order in which to add the different size beads, just remember this rule.

Row 7: You are going to decrease in this row to encourage the icing to spiral inwards as it continues to grow upwards. Pick up 1(B) and pass through 2 (C) from the previous row. Pick up 1 (C) and pass through the next (B) from the previous row. Repeat this another five times and step up at the end of the row. (Total 6(B) and 6(C) beads).

Row 8: this row confirms the decrease, so make sure you keep tight tension and pull the circle in as far as possible. Add 1(B), 1(C) all the way around the row and step up at the end. (total 6(B), 6(C) beads).

Rows 9 and 10: Repeat row 8.

Row 11: This is another decrease row. This time you will decrease in every third space. Remember to maintain the 'golden rule'. Pick up 1(B), pass through the next (C), pick up 1 (C), pass through the next (B), pick up 1(B), pass through the next (C) and the next (B). Repeat this

sequence twice more and step up at the end of the row, so you should exit from the first (B). (Total 6(B) and 3(C) beads).

Row 12: This is a straight row, so you will add 1(B), 1(C), 1(B). Repeat this sequence twice more. Be careful to pass through the correct beads from the previous row to ensure that you confirm the decrease. Remember to step up at the end of the row. (Total 6(B), 3(C) beads).

Row 13: This is another straight row, so repeat the same sequence you used in row 12. (Total 6(B), 3(C) beads).

Row 14: This is a decrease row. Pick up 1(B) and pass through the next (C) bead. Pick up 1(C) bead and pass through the next two (B) beads to make the decrease. Repeat this process twice more (notice how you are still following the 'golden rule'). Remember to step up at the end of the row to exit from your first (B) bead. (Total 3(B), 3(C) beads).

Row 15: This is a straight row. Add 1(B), 1(C), 1(B), 1(C), 1(B), 1(C) and step up at the end of the row. Again, take care to ensure that you confirm the decrease you made in the previous row – this can be tricky as you will be adding a size 11 (C) bead over the top of a pair of size 8 (B) beads, so you need to keep a really tight tension to pull the beads in as far as possible (total 3 (B), 3 (C) beads).

Row 16: Repeat row 15 and step up at the end. (Total 3(B), 3(C) beads).

Row 17: This is the final decrease row. Add 1(B) pass through the next (C) and the next (B). Repeat twice more and step up at the end of the row. (Total 3(B) beads).

Row 18: Add 1(B) bead in each space to confirm the decrease. Finally add a single (B) in the centre of this row to finish off the spiral. Finish off your thread and your cupcake is complete.

If you want to make a charm bracelet with these little treats, then use size 11 Delicas for the cake and size 11 seed beads for the (B) beads and size 15 seed beads for the (C) beads. You can attach a split ring to the top of the icing and then use this to attach to a charm bracelet. You can use a jump ring to link the charm to the bracelet.

Alternatively, make the sides of the cake, then continuing with your thread, add the icing before you add the base of the cake. When you have finished the icing and before you add the base, take a headpin, thread a size 8 (or slightly larger) bead onto this and then thread the pin through the centre of the top of the icing. Make a wrapped loop with the

pin. If you are very confident, then you can wrap this loop directly onto a link in the bracelet. This gives a neater finish than linking the charm and bracelet with a jump ring. The size 8 bead inside the icing should prevent the headpin from slipping through the top, so your charm will be secure. Add the base of the cake at the end to finish off.

Cupcake Charm Bracelet

Cupcake Earings
I made a pair of earrings to match my charm bracelet.

CHAPTER 8
MIXING BEAD SHAPES

These projects create cakes by mixing or joining together a combination of different Peyote stitch shapes.

The fondant fancies move seamlessly from a circular Peyote stitch shape to a square Peyote stitch shape in order to create the distinctive dome of cream that sits on top of the square cake base. **The simnel cake** uses a combination of triangular Peyote, tubular peyote and hexagon peyote in order to create the effect of a cake that has been sliced into. **The gingerbread men** are formed from a collection of pentagon, rectangles and circular Peyote to create their distinctive shape.

Fondant Fancies   page 90

Simnel Cake   page 94

Gingerbread Men   page 98

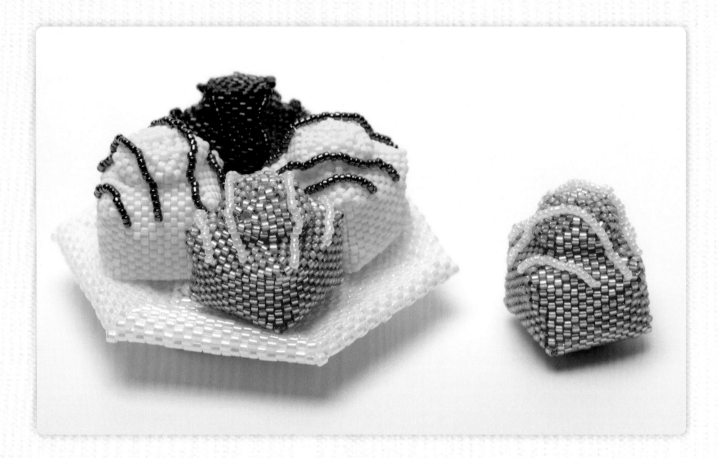

Fondant Fancies

Fondant Fancies, or French Fancies as they are sometimes known, are a British variety of iced sponge cake resembling Petit Fours. Originally produced by the Mr Kipling Cake Company, variations on these little treats are also now manufactured by other producers, although I believe the 'French Fancy' title remains copyrighted by Mr Kipling.

These cakes are a small cube shaped piece of sponge with a round dollop of vanilla flavoured cream on top. The whole structure is then covered with icing in either pink, yellow, or chocolate colour and decorated with strips of icing.

The bright colours of these cakes make a great display, but I was intrigued to try and replicate the mix of shapes required for this recipe. Integrating the round fondant top and the cube-shaped cake proved to be a mathematical challenge. The secret is all in the number of beads. The cube increase cycle works in multiples of twelve with an odd four to start out. The end of cycle one has 16 beads in a row, cycle two ends up with 28 beads in a row, etc. However, the circular increase cycle works in multiples of 6 (6, 12, 18, etc). If I was going to integrate the two shapes seamlessly, I needed to find a point at which each cycle contained the same number of beads per row. Unfortunately, because of the odd four at the start of the square cycle, this coincidence never occurs, so I had to cheat! Instead of increasing by 6 beads in the third circular increase cycle, I only increase by 4 beads, thus giving me 16 beads per row (instead of 18), from which point I could seamlessly convert to using the square increase cycle and thus the circular top would become the square base. Happily, the recipe is a lot simpler than it sounds! I'm dedicating this recipe to three school friends, Jenny, Melissa and Rachel, with thanks for their support.

INGREDIENTS

Per cake:
5g size 11 Delicas in one or each of the following colours: pink DB625, yellow DB751, brown DB709 (A)
1g size 15 seed beads in white (for pink cake), brown (for yellow cake), black (for brown cake) (B)
Thread to match or tone with your beads

Baking time: 90 minutes

RECIPE

This cake is made in two halves which are then joined together.

Start by making the top half of the cake. This starts with circular Peyote increase cycles and then converts to the square Peyote increase pattern.

Row 1: Pick up 3 (A) and tie them into a circle. You will stitch the tail thread in and finish it off at the end.

Row 2: Add 2 (A) between each bead in your base circle. This is an increase row. Remember to step up at the end of it (total 6 (A) beads).

Row 3: Add 1 (A) between each bead in row 2 and step up at the end (total 6 (A) beads).

Row 4: This is another increase row, so add 2 (A) between each bead in row 3 and step up at the end of the row (total 12 (A) beads).

Row 5 & 6: These are both straight rows, so just add 1 (A) between each bead in the previous row and step up at the end of the row (total 12 (A) beads).

Row 7: This is the 'cheat' row. It is an increase row, but instead of following the normal pattern of increasing in every other space, make your increase in the first, fourth, seventh and tenth spaces. You will stitch as follows: pick up 2 (A), pass through the next bead in row 6, pick up 1 (A), pass through the next bead in row 6, pick up 1 (A), pass through the next bead in row 6. Repeat this three more times to finish the row and step up at the end (total 16 (A) beads). You will notice that the increases in this row do not always sit over the increases in the previous increase cycle. Figure 1 shows your cake so far with the numbers representing each row number, so note how the increase beads line up.

FIGURE 1

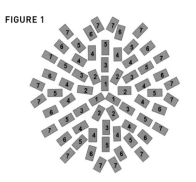

Rows 8-13: These are all straight rows, so just add one bead between each bead from the previous row and remember to step up at the end of each row (total 16 (A) beads). This will form the dome shape that sits on top of the cake.

Row 14: You are now going to start the square increase cycle so that the cake will flatten out again and become the top of the cube of sponge. Pick up 3 (A) and pass through the next bead in row 13, pick up 1 (A) and pass through the next bead in row 13, pick up 1 (A) and pass through the next bead in row 13, pick up 1 (A) and pass through the next bead in row 13. Repeat this three more times to take you to the end of the row and then step up (total 24 (A) beads). You should recognise that each space where you have added 3 beads is going to become a corner of your cube.

Row 15: This is the second row of the square increase cycle. In every space where you have added 3 beads in the previous row, you will be adding two beads (ie pass through the first bead in the group of three, pick up 2 and then pass through the last bead in the group of 3). In the intervening spaces you will add just one bead. Remember to step up at the end of the row (total 24 (A) beads).

Row 16: This is the third row in your square increase cycle, so you will be adding two beads in each corner space (ie between each pair of beads from the previous row). Remember to step up at the end of the row (total 28 (A) beads).

Row 17: This is the fourth row of your square increase cycle, so add 1 bead in every space (including the corners) and step up at the end (total 28 (A) beads).

Row 18: This is the fifth and final row of your square increase cycle, so add 1 bead in every space and step up at the end (total 28 (A) beads).

Rows 19-22: Instead of starting another increase cycle, you are now going to stitch four straight rows to start forming the sides of the cake. Remember to step up at the end of each row (total 28 (A) beads per row).

This completes the top half of your cake. Leave your working thread in case you need to use it for zipping up and put this half of the cake to one side. You may wish to finish off your tail thread at this point.

The bottom half of the cake is simply a straightforward square with sides built up.

Rows 1-12: Stitch 2 cycles of square increase. You will end up with 28 beads in your final row.

Rows 13-21: Stitch 9 straight rows to create the sides of the bottom half of the cake (total 28 (A) beads per row).

Add some material to stuff both halves of your cake to give it some structure – if you feel your stitching is strong enough for the cake to hold its shape naturally, then omit this step.

Carefully line up the top half and the bottom half of the cake to make sure that the corners on each half are in perfect alignment. You should find that you have an up bead in each corner on the bottom half and a down space in each corner on the top half, so the two halves will zip together perfectly. If this is not the case, then check the number of rows you have stitched – you may need to add an extra row to one of the halves. Before adding another row, check very carefully to make sure that the problem does lie with the number of rows and not with the way in which you have positioned the two halves.

To finish off your Fondant Fancy, use the (B) beads to add 5 strips of icing over the top of the cake. One strip should sit diagonally across the centre of the cake, with two strips on either side. Each strip should follow the shape of the cake, so that may mean stitching over the dome, or simply over the corner. Each strip should start and end near the top of one of the sides of the cake. Look at the photos here for guidance. If you have made a pink cake, then use white beads for the icing, a yellow cake uses brown beads and a brown cake uses black beads.

Fondant Fancy Fridge Magnet
I made a single cake into a fridge magnet

FIGURE 2

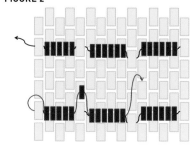

To stitch the strips, exit from a bead in the side of your cake, but near the top of the cube. Pick up between 5 and 7 (B) beads in the appropriate colour. Slide them along the thread so that they sit by the cake and lay them across the cake. Pass through a single bead on the cake as close as possible to the point at which the last bead is sitting. Pick up another few beads and repeat the process. Position your beads in the line of the stripe over the cake as you work, making sure that each new set of beads is going to continue a straight line following the contours of the cake (figure 2, top line). You will find that you have a break in the line at each point where you have passed through the cake. This will be filled in later on. When you reach the opposite side of the cake, pass through a cake bead to anchor the last strip of beads in place, then pass back through this final strip of (B) beads (figure 2, bottom line). Continue adding a single, or possibly two (B) to fill in each gap until your first strip of icing is complete. Pass your needle through the cake beads until you reach the point at which you wish to begin the next strip of icing. Add all five strips using the same technique.

Simnel Cake

The Simnel cake is a fruit cake with a layer of marzipan baked into its centre. It is then covered in toasted marzipan and traditionally decorated with 11 marzipan balls said to represent the true Apostles (excluding Judas). This cake dates back to Medieval times and there are various stories as to how it gained its name. Personally, I like the idea that it may have originated with a brother and sister (in some stories husband and wife) named Nell and Simon. The pair could not agree on how best to bake a cake for their mother – one wanted to bake the cake, the other to boil it – so they ended up doing both and creating this recipe. This cake has traditionally been eaten on the middle Sunday of Lent. More recently it became associated with Mothering Sunday – girls in service would make the cake to take home to their mother on this day. It can also be eaten on Easter Sunday when the end of Lent allows for the rich ingredients of this cake to be consumed once again.

The distinctive feature of a simnel cake is the layer of marzipan in the centre, but this is only visible once the cake has been cut. I decided to attempt the challenge of making a cake that had a slice cut from it. The hexagon shape that I had been using to make the top of cakes like the Victoria Sponge, is effectively six triangles. I realised I could make triangles and assemble them into a partial hexagon, to create the shape of a cake with a slice missing. This also allowed me to move into tubular Peyote to create the sides of the cake, so this project combines individual shapes to create a bigger whole. It also allows you the freedom to experiment with pattern as you create the fruit cake. I have not specified the exact patterning for the sides of the cake, but just given you a few ideas from which to work. If you want extra inspiration then study a real fruit cake or some photos of fruit cake. My Dad, who sadly passed away in 2006, loved Simnel cake, so this recipe is for him, with lots of love!

INGREDIENTS

Per Cake:
6g size 11 delicas DB751 for the marzipan (A)
4g size 11 Delicas DB709 for the cake (B)
2g size 11 Delicas DB734 for the raisins (C)
2g size 11 Delicas DB295 for the cherries (D)
6g size 11 Delicas DB231 for the plate (E)
10 6mm round beads in yellow to decorate the top
Optional two 4mm bead flowers
Thread to match or tone with your beads

Materials for the cake board

Baking time: 8 hours

RECIPE

You may want to try the recipe for Victoria sponge before attempting this recipe. This is a development of the slightly simpler Victoria Sponge in that the flat top for this cake is created from a collection of shapes, but after that, you will continue in Tubular Peyote to create the sides and use Circular Peyote again to make the plate.

The top is made from five Peyote Triangles that are 'zipped' together. Use the yellow (A) beads and work with a comfortable length of thread.

Triangle 1:

Row 1: pick up 3 beads and tie them into a circle, leaving a tail thread that you can stitch in later.

Row 2: add 2 (A) between each bead in row 1 and step up to exit from the first bead in your first pair of beads (total 6 (A) beads).

Row 3: add 2 (A) between each pair of beads – these form the corners of your triangle – and 1 (A) in each space along the sides. Step up to exit from the first bead in the first pair of beads (total 9 (A) beads).

Row 4: repeat row 3 (total 12 (A) beads).

Row 5: repeat row 3 (total 15 (A) beads).

Row 6: repeat row 3 (total 18 (A) beads).

Row 7: repeat row 3 (total 21 (A) beads).

Row 8: repeat row 3 (total 24 (A) beads).

Row 9: repeat row 3 (total 27 (A) beads).

Row 10: add a single (A) in each space, so just add a single bead in each corner instead of the pair of beads that you used in the previous increase rows. At the end of the row, finish off your thread and put the triangle to one side (total 27 (A) beads).

Triangles 2 to five are made in a similar manner, but on row 10 you will join these triangles to the previous triangle to form the shaped top of the cake.

Rows 1-9: repeat rows 1 to 9 exactly as you did for the first triangle.

Row 10: stitch along two sides of the triangle, so you will add a single bead in the first corner, stitch along the first side, add a single bead in the second corner, stitch along the second side and add a single bead in the third corner (total 19 (A) beads). Instead of adding new beads to the third side, line this side up with one of the sides on your first triangle and zip up the two sides. Finish off your thread. See figure 1.

FIGURE 1

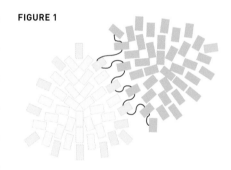

Make all subsequent triangles, zipping each one up to the side of the previous triangle so that you gradually form five sixths of a hexagon. See figure 2.

FIGURE 2

As you finish adding the fifth triangle, continue working a row of Peyote Stitch around the entire outside of the shape. You should be starting at the centre, so add a single bead between the inner corners of each triangle, then work along the side of one triangle, right around the outer edge of the cake, again adding a single bead in each space where the outer corners of the triangles

Fruit Cake Colouring

meet, and finally back along the side of the first triangle to step up and exit from the very first bead you added (total 71 (A) beads).

Rows 2-4: stitch 3 more rows of straight Peyote stitch right around the side of the cake, using the (A) beads. You should see the cake start to form into a tube and this completes the layer of marzipan on top of the cake (total 71 (A) beads per row).

Rows 5-13: the next nine rows are all straight Peyote stitch, but start adding the fruit cake colouring. The pattern for this is free form, but you want to think about creating the effect of a real fruit cake. I used the (B) beads to represent the cake, the (C) beads for the raisins and the (D) beads for the cherries. I tried to create the effect of raisins and cherries dotted throughout the cake by adding groups of three or four (C) or (D) beads to represent the fruit within the cake. Figure 3 gives you some ideas as to how you might achieve this effect.

Each row contains 71 beads in total, but the mix of colours will depend on your choice.

FIGURE 3

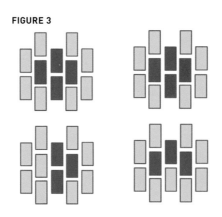

Rows 14 & 15: in these rows you need to add the marzipan in the centre of the cake. In the 'V' shape stitch (A) beads, but maintain the fruitcake pattern round the rest of the cake. The marzipan does not extend to the edge of the cake, so start adding the (A) beads in the second space in the 'V' and stop in the equivalent position on the other side.

Rows 16-24: repeat rows 5-13 to add the bottom half of the cake.

You will now start adding the plate, but first you need to add the part of plate that sits under the space where the cake has been cut. Use the (E) beads and make another triangle.

Rows 1-9: repeat the same pattern as you used to make the first triangles for the top of the cake.

Row 10: stitch another increase row, so add a pair of beads in each corner, but single beads along the sides of the triangle (total 30 (E) beads).

Row 11: stitch along one side of the triangle, adding 1 (E) in each space, then zip up the other two sides to the bottom row of the 'V' of the cake.

Simnel Cake Fridge Magnet
A slice of Simnel cake makes a great fridge magnet or key ring.

You are now ready to add the plate. This is the same method as you used when making the Victoria Sponge, using the (E) beads and a hexagonal Peyote increase pattern.

Row 1: add a pair of (E) beads in the space where the plate joins the cake on each side of the cake, then add a pair of beads in each tenth space as you work around the cake. You will have made an increase in six places to form the six evenly spaced corners of the hexagon shape. Remember to step up at the end of the row (total 68 (E) beads).

Rows 2 & 3: these are straight rows, but remember to step up at the end of each row (total 68 (E) beads).

Row 4: this is an increase row – add a pair of beads in each of the corner spaces and step up at the end of the row (total 74 (E) beads).

Rows 5 & 6: stitch two more straight rows and step up at the end of each row (total 74 (E) beads).

Row 7: stitch your final increase row (total 80 (E) beads).

Add the cardboard base backing (see page 29) and stitch another four or five straight rows using the (E) beads to cover the base and finish your cake.

To add the decoration on the top, stitch 10 6mm round yellow beads at equal intervals around the cake. You will only use 10 as the 11th ball would be on the slice of cake that is missing. I also added a couple of tiny bead flowers in the centre of the cake.

This cake also lends itself to being made as a slice to turn into a key ring or fridge magnet. As with the other cake slices for the Victoria Sponge and Chocolate Gateau, make two halves and zip them up. Follow the recipe above, but just make a single triangle and continue stitching down the sides until you reach the half way point, where the marzipan is added. Make the bottom half by making a triangle using all the cake beads and following the pattern for incorporating raisins and cherries. Continue stitching up the sides of the triangle and when you reach the final row before the marzipan, stuff both halves and zip them up. Add a single round bead to the top for the marzipan ball. Attach a fridge magnet or key ring finding.

Gingerbread Men

Gingerbread has a long tradition dating back to the ancient world. Ginger root comes from Malaysia and was traditionally used to soothe upset stomachs and prevent colds. Throughout pre-Christian Europe, the Winter Solstice was celebrated with small gingerbread cakes adorned with the symbol of the sun. Soldiers returning from the Crusades brought back the ingredients for the traditional gingerbread recipe: ginger, sugars, almonds and citrus fruits. The recipe we would recognise today emerged in around 1300 when English cooks began adding breadcrumbs to the mixture.

During Medieval times, gingerbread became so popular that many festivities were known as 'Gingerbread Fairs', giving rise to an alternative name for the biscuit: Fairings, to denote a gift given or bought at a fair.

Recipes for gingerbread and ginger cake varied from country to country throughout Europe and the USA, but, arguably, Germany developed the strongest tradition for this little biscuit. During the nineteenth-century, gingerbread men became increasingly associated with Christmas. In the UK, this reflected the influence of Prince Albert's German traditions, combined with the increasing commercialisation of Christmas.

The idea for this little treat came from Shanika. It is a wonderfully distinctive idea, but took me a lot of thought to develop! I ended up breaking the traditional gingerbread man into a collection of basic shapes, stitching each and then joining them together as a whole to form the gingerbread man. This recipe makes great ever-lasting Christmas ornaments. Alternatively, made up in size 15 beads, it can be worn as a pendant. This is for Shanika with thanks for an idea that pushed my boundaries and for a great friendship. To shared memories!

INGREDIENTS

Per gingerbread man:

7g size 11 Delicas in DB709 (A)
6 size 10 Delicas in DB201 for decoration (B)
7 size 11 Delicas in in your choice of colour for the tie (C)
7 size 15 seed beads in Ceylon white for the mouth (D)
Optional for the hat:
1g size 11 Matsuno seed beads in red
1g size 15 seed beads in Ceylon white
3 size 10 Delicas in DB201

Thread to match or tone with your beads
French wire and 12mm split ring

Baking time: 2 hours

Gingerbread Man Pendant
I made a pendant using size 15 beads
for the gingerbread man, size 11 Delicas
for the buttons, eyes and nose and
size 15 beads for the bow tie and mouth.

RECIPE

Each little man is made from separate components – head, body, arms, legs – that are stitched together to form the shape. You will in effect make two men, add decoration to one and leave the other plain, then zip the two together so that the finished piece holds its form. This recipe uses Peyote stitch rectangles, square and also hexagon, so make sure you are familiar with the increase pattern for all those shapes before you start out.

Start by making the body. This starts out as a square, but then adds a hexagon increase pattern to the bottom end so that the shaping for adding the legs is formed.

Row 1: pick up 4 (A) and tie them into a circle, leaving a 6" tail thread that you can use to add the decoration.

Row 2: add 1 (A) between each of the beads in row 1 and step up at the end of the row (total 4 (A) beads).

Row 3: add 3 (A) between each of the beads in the previous row and step up through the first bead (total 12 (A) beads).

Row 4: add a pair of (A) beads in each corner and 1 (A) bead along each side, following the square increase cycle pattern (total 12 (A) beads).

Row 5: add a pair of (A) beads in each corner and 2 (A) beads along each side, following the square increase cycle pattern. Step up at the end of the row (total 16 (A) beads).

Row 6: this is a straight row, so add 16 (A) beads and step up at the end of the row.

Row 7: this is the second straight row that completes your first square increase cycle. Step up at the end of the row (total 16 (A) beads).

Row 8: this is an increase row. On the bottom half of your square you will be following a hexagon increase pattern. On the top half of your square you will follow the square increase pattern. Add single beads along the first side, when you reach the first corner, add a pair of beads, then add 1 (A) bead, add a pair of (A) beads – this will be in the centre of your bottom side – add 1 (A) bead and add a pair of (A) beads in the second corner. Add single (A) beads along the third side of your square, add 3 (A) beads in the third corner. Add single (A) beads along the fourth side and 3 (A) beads in the fourth corner. Step up at the end of the row (total 23 (A) beads). See figure 1.

FIGURE 1

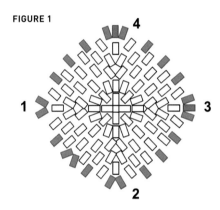

Row 9: In this row you will add 1 (A) in each space along the side. Add 1 (A) in between each pair of beads that you added in corners 1 and 2 and along the second side. Add 2 (A) in corners three and four, following the square increase pattern. Step up at the end of the row (total 23 (A) beads).

Row 10: this is a straight row, so add a single bead in every space (total 23 (A) beads). At the end of the row, finish off your thread.

You should find that the bottom of the body has a slight point to it where you have made the hexagon increase. This is to allow the legs to sit at a slight angle. The arms will attach immediately below the top two corners, on the side at a ninety degree angle.

Add the buttons and bow tie, placing them as shown.

Using your tail thread, add the buttons to the body. Add 1 (B) bead in the very centre of the body. Add a second (B) bead immediately below the first, about 3 rows down. Add a third (B) bead about three rows above the centre button. Pass your thread up to exit from the centre bead in the outer row at the top of the body. Pick up 1 (C) and pass through the bead in the body. Pass through the (C) bead again. Pick up 3 (C) and pass through the original (C). This forms one half of the bow tie. Pick up 3 (C) and pass through the original (C) again. The green beads in figure 2 illustrate the bow tie. It should sit directly on top of the top body beads. Take your thread back down into the body beads and finish it off.

FIGURE 2

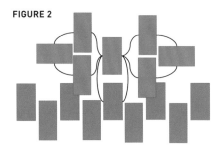

Next make the legs. These are made as a rectangle using the half square increase cycle.

Rows 1 & 2: pick up 9 (A). Leave a tail that you can stitch in later and you may also want to use a stop bead to prevent the beads from falling off your thread as you work the next row.

Rows 3 - 5: Work odd count Peyote stitch with 5(A) in row 3, 4 (A) in row 4 and 5 (A) in row 5.

Row 6: add 4 (A) along the first side. When you get to the end, add 3 (A) along

the end and then stitch back down the second side, adding another 3 (A) at the other end. Step up to exit from the first bead you added (total 14 (A) beads).

Row 7: add a single (A) in each space along the side, add 3 (A) in each corner and a single (A) in the centre of the three end beads. Step up at the end of the row (total 20 (A) beads).

Row 8: add single beads in every space along the straight edges and a pair of beads in each corner (total 20 (A) beads).

Row 9: this is a straight row, so add a bead in every space (total 20 (A) beads). When you finish the row, take your thread to exit from one of the next corner beads. Hold your leg so that its short side will zip up with one of the bottom sides of the body. Make sure that the corner of the leg aligns with the central bead that forms the slight point on the bottom of the body. Zip the two shapes together and finish off all your threads.

FIGURE 3

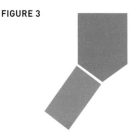

Make a second leg and attach it to the other side of the bottom of the body.

Next make the two arms. They are also made as a Peyote stitch rectangle, but this time you will start with just 5 beads.

Rows 1 & 2: pick up 5 (A) beads. Again, leave a tail thread that you can stitch in and use a stop bead if necessary.

Row 3: total 3 (A) beads.

Row 4: total 2 (A) beads.

Row 5: total 3 (A) beads.

Row 6: this is the row in which you add the three beads at the end. Total 10 (A) beads

Row 7: you will be adding 3 beads in each corner, a single bead along each side and at each end, (total 16 (A) beads).

Row 8: add a pair of beads in each corner and single beads along all the sides (total 16 (A) beads).

Row 9: this is a straight row, so add single beads in each space and at each corner. Total 20 (A) beads). When you finish the row take your needle through to exit from the next corner bead. Attach the arm to the body immediately below the top corner so that it sits at a ninety degree angle to the body.

FIGURE 4

Make a second arm and attach it to the other side of the body.

The head is made as a Peyote stitch hexagon and then decorated.

Row 1: pick up 3 (A) and tie them into a circle. Leave a tail thread of about 6" that you can use to add the decoration.

Row 2: add 2 (A) in every space – total 6 (A) beads.

Row 3: add 1 (A) between each bead in row 2 – total 6 (A) beads.

Row 4: add 2 (A) in each space – total 12 (A) beads.

Row 5: add 1 (A) between every bead in row 4 – total 12 (A) beads.

Row 6: add 1 (A) in each space – total 12 (A) beads.

Row 7: add 1 (A) in the first space, 2 (A) in the second space, continue this pattern round the rest of the row - total 18 (A) beads.

Row 8: add 1 (A) between each bead in row 7 – total 18 (A) beads.

Row 9: add 1 (A) in each space – total 18 (A) beads.

Row 10: add 2 (A) in the first space, 1 (A) in the second space, 1 (A) in the third space and repeat this pattern to the end of the row. Now attach the head to the body. Align the beads so that they will zip up and make sure that the head is sitting in the centre of the top of the body. If you have a long length of thread left, then leave it as you will be able to use it for the final step.

Return to the tail thread and use it to add the features to the face.

Add 1 (B) in the centre of the head to make the nose. Add 2 (B) just above the centre and slightly to either side to make the eyes. To add the mouth, take your thread to exit from a bead that is directly underneath the nose, about 3 rows down from the centre. Pick up 1 (D), pass through the next adjacent bead in the head, *pick up 1 (D) and pass through the next adjacent bead in the head. You should be following the path of a row of head beads so that the mouth will curve upwards into a smile. Pick up 1 (D) and pass back through the second (D) you added. Pick up 1 (D) and pass back through the first (D). Repeat from * going in the opposite direction to add the other half of the mouth. Pass through all the mouth beads a couple more times so that they form a curved line. You can play around and use your own imagination to add different expressions to the faces of these little men, so try experimenting a little and if you are struggling to understand the way in which I have added the mouth, just invent your own method.

Add eyes, nose and mouth,
positioning them as shown.

The final step is to add a row of Peyote stitch right around the entire of the outside of your gingerbread man. This will allow you to zip together the front and back halves later on. Either return to the thread you were using to make

the head, or begin a new thread and add a bead in every space working your way around the outside of the entire shape. You will probably find that you need to add two beads in the spaces at the shoulders and hips. When you are working round the head, you will notice that your final head row included several pairs of beads. Pass through the pair each time you add a bead, do not add a bead in between each pair. This will help to give the head a more rounded shape. Finish off all your threads and put this front half of your gingerbread man to one side.

Make a second half following all these instructions again, but this time, do not add any decoration. This will be the back of your gingerbread man. When it is complete, hold the front half and back half together and you should find that you can use the additional row you added round the outside on the front half, to zip up the back half and give your gingerbread man a substantial form. You can add a split ring to the top of his head and attach a length of ribbon to hang him on the Christmas tree. Alternatively, he can be used as a pendant, key ring or handbag charm. Just attach the appropriate finding.

If you want to add the Father Christmas hat, this is made as a Peyote triangle in two halves and then attached to the head. The split ring can then be attached to the top of the hat.

For the hat, you will need to use size 11 Matsuno seed beads as these are just slightly larger than the Delicas and will allow you to sit the hat on the head.

Row 1: pick up 3 beads and tie them into a circle.

Row 2: add 2 beads between each of the beads in row 1. Step up to exit from the first bead in your first pair (total 6 beads).

Row 3: pick up 2 beads and pass through the second bead in this pair. Pick up 1 bead and pass through the first bead in your next pair. Repeat to the end of the row and step up through the first bead in your first pair (total 9 beads).

Row 4: add a pair of beads in each pair from row 3 and a single bead along each of the sides. You should see that the pairs of beads are forming the corners of your triangle. Step up through the first bead in your first pair at the end of the row (total 12 beads).

Row 5: add a pair of beads in each corner and a single bead in each space along the sides (total 15 beads).

Row 6: add a pair of beads in each corner and a single bead in each space along the sides (total 18 beads).

Row 7: stitch along the first two sides, but add a single bead in each space, so omit the increases in the corners. On the third side, do not add any beads, just stitch this side to the top of the head, making sure that the two sides of the hat sit slightly outside the edge of the head. See figure 5.

FIGURE 5

Make the back side of the hat in exactly the same way, but when you reach row 7, instead of adding any extra beads, zip up this half to the half that is already on your gingerbread man: use the beads from row 7 on the first half of your hat to stitch along two of the sides and stitch the third side (bottom) to the back of your man's head. Add fur trim round the bottom row of the hat using size 15 seed beads: pick up 2 size 15, pass through the next red bead and so on right around the hat. Step up to exit from the first pair of size 15s. Pick up 2 more size 15 and pass through the next pair of white beads – continue round the rest of the hat. You will find that the beads pucker up rather than lying flat. This gives the effect of fur. Add three size 10 white Delicas to the top of the hat and attach the split ring to these Delicas to finish off your Christmas decoration.

SUPPLIERS

I have purchased all of the beads used in these recipes from the following suppliers.

Charisma Beads

Shop located in Hitchin in Hertfordhsire. I purchased size 10 Delicas from here.

www.charismabeads.co.uk

GJ Beads

Warehouse located in St Erth and shops located in Truro and St Ives, Cornwall. I sourced the Matsuno seed beads and size 11 Delicas from here.

www.gjbeads.co.uk

Spellbound Bead Company

Shop located in Lichfield, Staffordshire. I purchased Delicas from here.

www.spellboundbead.co.uk

The London Bead Company

Shop located in Kentish Town Road, London. This is an excellent source for Delicas in a huge range of colours.

www.londonbeadco.co.uk

Thank you for sharing my journey.
Wishing you many happy hours of beading and baking!
Best Wishes,
Katie